BAKER'S SECRET

JULIA AITKEN'S
BAKER'S SECRET
QUICK & EASY BAKING

Grosvenor House Press Inc.
Toronto~Montréal

Published with the cooperation of Ekco Canada Inc., the manufacturers of Baker's Secret Non-Stick Bakeware.

The publishers wish to thank Ekco Canada Inc. for a grant which has helped to make possible the publication of this book.

Baker's Secret is a registered trademark of **EKCO** Canada Inc.

Canadian Cataloguing in Publication Data
   Aitken, Julia, 1955–
   Julia Aitken's baker's secret

   Includes index.
   ISBN 0-919959-27-X

   1. Baking. I. Title. II. Title: Baker's secret.

   TX763.A47 1986   641.7'1   C86-093620-1

Published by

Grosvenor House Press Inc.
111 Queen Street East
Suite 375
Toronto, Ontario
M5C 1S2

Éditions Grosvenor
Passage du musée
1456 rue Sherbrooke ouest
3ième Étage
Montréal, Québec
H3G 1K4

Printed and bound in Canada
Illustrations by Shelagh Armstrong and Bob Paul
Photography by Simon Cheung
Food styling by Olga Truchan and Rosemarie Strathdee
Cover design by David Sutherland
Interior book design by Graphicmen Incorporated

TABLE OF CONTENTS

AUTHOR'S ACKNOWLEDGEMENTS

No book, especially a cookbook, is the product of just one person. There are many 'unsung heroes' behind the scenes of whom I should like to sing. Grateful thanks and appreciation go to the following people:

To my mother, who inspired me to cook in the first place and from whom I inherited my enthusiasm for food; to Linda Fisher, who typed the original manuscript for this book perfectly and without complaint, despite the impossible deadlines I imposed on her; to Bev Renehan, who patiently and meticulously edited the manuscript and helped me smooth out the wrinkles; to Linda Szostak, who equally carefully copy edited my prose; to Olga Truchan and Rosemarie Strathdee who worked their food styling magic on my recipes and dressed them up in their best for photography; to Simon Cheung, food photographer 'extraordinaire', whose exquisite photographs bring the recipes to life; and to Grosvenor House Press, for giving me the wonderful opportunity to write this book.

At the end of my list, but not of my thoughts, many thanks to my husband, Iain, for his constant encouragement and support. Despite possessing a decidedly un-sweet tooth, he manfully munched his way through each and every recipe in this book to ensure that it passed the taste test. It is to Iain that this book is dedicated.

Baker's Secret Baking Pans by EKCO

1

INTRODUCTION

"To stir butter and sugar is the hardest part of cake making. Have this done by a manservant."

from Miss Leslie's New Cookery Book
by E. Leslie, 1857

Sadly, for lazybones like me, the days of having your own personal manservant have long gone. The ones on two legs have been replaced, however, by those on four little rubber feet — the electric mixer and all those other wonders of modern science that grace our kitchens.

An electric mixer beats fluffy lightness into a cake in seconds and baking powder adds to the rise without the elbow grease. Quick-rising yeast makes bread-baking a snap. Food processors chop ingredients (or if your back is turned, pulverize them to mush) at an amazing rate. They also make the best pastry in the world.

Baking, that homey, cosy pastime that's been with us for centuries, has finally come of age. It's no longer arm-breaking hard work. It's fast, it's simple and, even better, it's fun.

A new style of baking requires a new type of cookbook. Bakers in the '80s need speedy, easy-to-follow recipes that let home-baking slot happily into hectic schedules.

Today's bakers also require streamlined baking equipment to help cut corners at cleanup time. There are many good quality, nonstick pans on the market and I can highly recommend Baker's Secret Baking Pans by Ekco. These pans have a durable silicone coating, both inside and out, which ensures that even the stickiest home-bakes slide out quickly and easily, making washing up a snap.

Whether you commute to work every day or are a busy homemaker, you'll have time for the home-bakes in this book. The recipes have been developed (much to the detriment of my waistline) to shave minutes off both preparation and cleanup time. They use readily available ingredients and, as a bonus, they taste delicious, too.

I find cooking — baking in particular — to be a wonderful form of therapy. Nothing relieves tension more effectively than venting your frustrations on an inanimate lump of dough. You can pound away on bread dough to your heart's content without doing any damage. Go easy, though, on pastry and cookie dough or it will get back at you by becoming tough in the oven (for more on this, see First Aid, p. 24).

The best part of this "baking therapy", however, is that so little time and effort produces such a satisfying end result. It's no accident that these days so many air fresheners and room deodorants are made to smell like freshly baked apple pie or spices. Such evocative scents waft from the oven during baking and, when the piping hot cake or bread is removed and left to cool, that warm, cozy aroma makes you feel all is right with the world.

Set aside 30 minutes or so from your busy day. That's the very most you'll need to rustle up some crisp cookies, a fruity quick bread or a rich chocolate cake. Then, sit back and enjoy the fruits of your labors, for tomorrow we diet!

BEFORE YOU BEGIN

Whether you're an old hand when it comes to baking or a nervous beginner, it's wise to organize a little before you launch into a recipe, especially if it's something you haven't tried before.

1 Read through the recipe from start to finish. Check that you have all the ingredients and utensils required.

2 Assemble all the ingredients and utensils (including baking pans), and preheat the oven, if necessary. If you lead a hectic lifestyle and are likely to be interrupted mid-recipe (by children, phone or doorbell), it's a good idea to return each ingredient to the cupboard or refrigerator as you measure and add it to the mixing bowl. That way, when you return to your mixing, you'll know exactly which ingredients have been added.

3 Go through the recipe step-by-step, following the instructions carefully. Most baking mixtures don't like to be kept waiting so transfer them to nonstick or lightly greased baking pans, then put them in the oven as quickly as possible, unless the recipe tells you otherwise.

4 Once your cake, quick bread or cookies are in the oven, clean up any mess (remember, a messy cook is a creative cook — that's my excuse, anyway!). Prepare any frosting or decoration that's required for the finished product.

5 Check on your home-bake after the minimum baking time specified in the recipe. If no minimum time is mentioned, check on it a couple of minutes before the cooking time expires, especially if experience has taught you that your oven is hotter than average. Open the door slowly, especially when checking a cake, as a sudden rush of cold air could make a perfectly risen cake fall. Test your home-bake for doneness as indicated in the recipe. As a rough guide:
- cake should shrink away from the sides of the pan and the top should spring back when pressed gently. A skewer inserted in the center should come out clean.
- muffins, quick breads and tea biscuits should be well risen and golden brown.
- cookies should be firm to touch and tinged with gold.
- breads and rolls should be well risen and golden brown and should sound hollow when tapped on the bottom.

6 Let cool as indicated in the recipe and decorate, if necessary.

THE TOOLS OF THE TRADE

From the simplest of cookies to the gooeyest of gâteaux, if your kitchen is equipped with the "basics" you can make any of the recipes in this book. Here's a quick checklist of everything you'll need.

- **Aluminum foil**
- **Baking Pans:**
  small and large cookie sheets
  12-cup muffin pan
  12-cup tartlet pan
  7-1/2 × 3-1/2-inch (3 cup/750 mL) loaf pan
  8-1/2 × 4-1/2-inch (6 cup/1.5 L) loaf pan
  8-inch (20 cm) round cake pan
  13- × 9- × 1/2-inch (33 × 23 × 1.25 cm) jelly roll pan
  8-3/4-inch (22 cm) pie plate
  11- × 7-inch (28 × 18 cm) cake pan
  8-inch (20 cm) square cake pan
- **Blender* and/or food processor***
- **Bowl scraper** (nylon)
- **Cake server** (nylon)
- **Cake tester* or skewer**
- **Can opener**
- **Chopping board**
- **Cookie cutters:**
  2-inch (5 cm)
  3-inch (7.5 cm)
  3-1/2-inch (9 cm)
- **Double boiler*** (or you can use a bowl standing over a pan of simmering water)
- **Electric mixer**
- **Food processor* and/or blender***
- **Forks**
- **Freezer bags**
- **Graters:**
  cheese
  nutmeg*

- **Icing bag with writing and star tips**
- **Juicer**
- **Measuring cups**
- **Measuring spoons**
- **Metal spoons of various sizes**
- **Mixing bowls:**
  small
  medium
  large
- **Paper baking cups**
- **Paper towels**
- **Pastry blender**
- **Pastry brush**
- **Plastic wrap**
- **Rolling pin**
- **Ruler**
- **Saucepans:**
  small
  medium
  large
  (including a heavy one for melting sugar)
- **Sieve**
- **Sifter***
- **Skewer or cake tester***
- **Spatula** (nylon)
- **Tea towels**
- **Toothpicks**
- **Waxed paper**
- **Whisk**
- **Wire racks**
- **Wooden spoons of various sizes**

*not absolutely essential

BACK TO BASICS

What makes baking such fun is that many home-bakes can be whipped up by using items in your cupboard. Here are a few helpful hints about some of the ingredients used in this book.

Butter:
Salted butter is used throughout the book. Use it straight from the refrigerator unless the recipe specifies "at room temperature". However, in very hot or humid weather, use butter straight from the refrigerator in all recipes. The verdict of the butter versus margarine debate comes down to personal preference but I recommend butter for cookies and butter-cream frosting. For shortbread, there is simply no substitute.

Brown Sugar:
This adds a toffee flavor and attractive color to home-bakes but easily goes hard in the package if it is not stored in a cool, dry place. If your brown sugar turns as hard as concrete, heat it, uncovered, in a 200°F (100°C) oven until it's dry and crumbly, then process it in a food processor.

Cayenne Pepper:
This is a very hot spice which is to be used sparingly. Don't confuse it with paprika pepper which is the same color but, generally, very mild.

Cocoa Powder:
The unsweetened variety is used throughout the book.

Cream:
Whipping (35%) cream is used throughout the book.

Cumin:
This is a pungent spice popular in Indian cuisine.

Eggs:
Large eggs are used throughout the book. If only yolks are needed in a recipe, don't throw the rest of the egg away. Store the whites in a covered container in the refrigerator for up to four days. Cover the yolks carefully with water, cover the container and store it in the refrigerator for up to two days. Both whites and yolks can be frozen but are best frozen separately. They keep for up to 6 months. Pack whites in a covered container and label it with the date. Yolks must be mixed with *either* salt *or* sugar, depending on whether they'll be used for savory or sweet dishes (1 tsp/5 mL salt *or* 2 tsp/10 mL sugar for every 6 yolks). Pack them in a covered container and label it clearly so you know whether yolks are salted or sugared.

Extracts:

These are very concentrated essences used to impart the taste of vanilla, brandy, peppermint, etc. to cakes, pastries and desserts. Use them sparingly. An *extract* gives a more authentic taste than a *flavoring*, so check the label on the bottle carefully.

Feta Cheese:

A salty, crumbly white goat cheese, it's sold in cartons in most supermarkets.

Flour:

All-purpose:
Apart from the "Wholly Delicious" chapter (p. 71), in which baking with whole wheat flour is highlighted, all-purpose flour is used throughout the book. As its name implies, all-purpose flour is suitable for all types of baking and gives the best results, especially if you're a beginner.
Semolina:
A coarse, cream-colored flour ground from durum wheat, it adds richness to shortbreads.
Whole Wheat:
Unrefined flour, rich in iron and vitamin B, you should never sift whole wheat flour.

Food Coloring:

Always buy food coloring from the supermarket, don't experiment by making your own! It's very concentrated so mix a few drops at a time into a recipe until you've achieved the shade you want.

Garam Masala:

This is a blend of herbs and spices used as the main seasoning in curries. It is available, ready-mixed, in large supermarkets and delicatessens.

Herbs:

Fresh herbs have a finer flavor but, for baking, dried herbs give just as good results. If you want to substitute fresh herbs for dried in any of the recipes, you'll need about twice the specified amount, as fresh herbs are milder.

Margarine:

In recipes that require fats to be used "at room temperature", soft margarine in a tub can be used straight from the refrigerator.

Milk:

All the recipes were tested with 2%, but homogenized would work just as well.

Nutmeg:

Always buy whole nutmegs and grate the spice freshly every time you need it.

Nuts:
For freshness, always buy nuts in small quantities and in sealed packages. Stale nuts can taste quite rancid and certainly don't improve a recipe.

Raising Agents:
These include baking powder, baking soda and cream of tartar. Always use the one specified in the recipe.

Rolled Oats:
Any variety — quick, instant or slow-cook — can be used in baking.

Shortening:
This is the best choice of fat for pastry and breads.

Yeast:
Quick-rising, active dried yeast is recommended for speedy baking.

BAKING IN THE CLOUDS

Just a quick word to all you alpine bakers out there — those who spend baking day above 2,500 feet.

Since doughs and cake batters rise faster the higher you are, oven temperatures must be increased. From 2,500 to 7,500 feet above sea level, raise the oven temperature stated in the recipe by 10 to 15°F (6 to 9°C). Reduce each teaspoonful (5 mL) baking powder by 1/8 to 1/4 tsp (0.5 to 1 mL).

The amount of sugar must also be reduced. Between 2,500 and 5,000 feet, reduce each 1 cup (250 mL) sugar by 1 to 2 tbsp (15 to 25 mL). Between 5,000 and 7,000 feet, reduce each 1 cup (250 mL) by 2 to 3 tbsp (25 to 45 mL).

To compensate for faster rising, the liquid content of a recipe must be increased. Between 2,500 and 5,000 feet, each 1 cup (250 mL) liquid should be increased by 1 to 3 tbsp (15 to 45 mL). Between 5,000 and 7,000 feet, each 1 cup (250 mL) should be increased by 2 to 4 tbsp (25 to 45 mL).

A little experimentation is necessary and if problems arise, you should seek the advice of a local home economist.

HOW DO YOU MEASURE UP?

Accurate measuring of ingredients is essential to successful baking, so, unless you're an absolute tried and true expert, use a good set of measuring spoons and cups. Both imperial and metric measurements are given in the recipes but use one or the other, never mix the two in the same recipe.

To measure dry ingredients:
Spoon into measuring cup until heaped, then draw a knife across the top of the cup to level surface.

To measure brown sugar:
Pack firmly into measuring cup until surface is level with top of cup or to required level.

To measure liquids:
Fill measuring cup to the brim or to required level.

To measure syrup, honey and other sticky substances:
Dip measuring cup in flour first before filling. Measuring cup will be easier to empty.

To measure fats:
Pack firmly in measuring cup until heaped, then draw a knife across the top of the cup to level surface.

To measure fats for melting:
Estimate amount by filling measuring cup roughly. Measure again once fat is melted.

WHAT RECIPES MEAN WHEN THEY SAY . . .

All the recipes in this book are very straightforward but if you come across an unfamiliar phrase, just check this glossary of cooking terms.

Batter:
Usually a smooth, liquid combination of flour, eggs and milk but when used to describe a cake mixture, refers to a slightly thicker, sauce-like consistency.

Beat:
To mix ingredients with quick, circular strokes. Beating adds air and makes mixture lighter and fluffier. An electric mixer is usually the best utensil to use — it saves time and energy.

Blend:
To mix ingredients until smooth.

Boil:
To heat liquid until bubbling (212°F/100°C).

Chop:
To cut into small pieces.

Coat the back of a spoon:
Usually refers to custards or icings. When mixture is of the right consistency, a spoon dipped in should come out evenly and easily coated.

Combine:
To mix two or more ingredients thoroughly.

Core:
To remove central core from apples, pears, etc.

Cream:
To soften one, two or more ingredients by pressing them against the side of a bowl with the back of a spoon and beating until smooth and creamy. Usually refers to butter alone, or butter and sugar.

Crumble:
To break up with fingers.

Crush:
To reduce to crumbs either by pounding with a rolling pin or by processing in a food processor or coffee grinder.

Dredge:
To sprinkle work surface or food evenly with flour or icing sugar to coat completely.

Drizzle:
To trickle a liquid substance (e.g. honey or glacé icing) in a thin stream over food.

Drop:
To let fall from a spoon in small heaps. Usually refers to cookie dough.

Dust:
To sprinkle lightly with flour or icing sugar.

Firm up:
To allow freshly baked cookies to harden slightly before removing them from cookie sheets.

Firmly packed:
Describes the method of measuring brown sugar. It must be firmly pressed into the measuring cup to yield correct quantity.

Fold in:
To mix with a gentle over-and-under motion by cutting through ingredients with a spoon and bringing bottom ingredients to top. Used when mixing light ingredients, such as whisked egg whites or whipped cream, into a heavier one, such as a cake batter. Folding in retains the mixture's lightness. It's best to use a metal spoon.

Glaze:
To give food a shiny appearance by brushing with honey, syrup or, before baking, beaten egg.

Grate:
To shred food by rubbing against a grater.

Grease:
To rub with fat or oil.

Ground:
Describes food, such as nuts or spices, reduced to very fine particles.

Hull:
To remove leaves and stem from fruit, such as strawberries.

Invert:
To turn upside down.

Knead:
To fold dough over on itself, press and turn with your hands to make it smooth and free of cracks.

Mash:
To press or beat an ingredient with a fork or potato masher until smooth and creamy.

Paste:
A smooth, sticky, blended mixture.

Pinch:
Amount of dried ingredients, such as salt, spices or herbs that can be held between your finger and thumb.

Pipe:
To force mixture through an icing bag.

Pit:
To remove stones or pits from fruits, such as prunes, olives, cherries.

Preheat:
To bring oven to correct temperature, before cooking food.

Process:
To change the consistency of an ingredient, using a food processor.

Purée:
A smooth, thick mixture made by rubbing one or more ingredients through a sieve or by processing them in a blender or food processor. Also describes this process.

Roll out:
To roll to a thin, flat sheet, using a rolling pin.

Rub in:
To thoroughly mix two or more ingredients (usually flour and fat) by rubbing them between your thumbs and fingertips or by using a pastry blender.

Score:
To make shallow cuts with a knife.

Sift:
To pass dry ingredients, such as flour, baking powder, etc. through a sifter or sieve to remove lumps and combine them thoroughly.

Simmer:
To heat liquid until bubbles begin to form (approximately 185°F/89°C).

Slivered:
Usually describes nuts, such as almonds, that are cut into strips rather than chopped.

Soft, dropping consistency:
Describes a cake batter that drops from a spoon in dollops.

Soft peaks:
Usually describes cream that has been whipped until, when whisk is lifted, cream forms peaks that turn over slightly at top instead of standing straight.

Stiff peaks:
Usually describes egg whites that have been whisked until, when whisk is lifted, egg whites form peaks that stand straight.

Stir:
To mix with a slower, smoother motion than beating. Unlike beating, stirring doesn't incorporate air into a mixture.

Whip:
To beat very vigorously with a wire whisk or electric mixer to incorporate air into an ingredient to add bulk and fluffiness. Usually refers to cream.

Whisk:
Same as above but usually refers to egg whites.

WHAT'S IN STORE

The golden rule of baking is that a home-bake is only as good as the items that go into it. Poor quality or stale ingredients produce an inferior cake. To ensure *your* home-bakes are perfectly delicious, check this handy storage guide to see just how long those cupboard standbys keep. Some of the times may surprise you.

Cupboard Storage	Keeps This Long
Dry Goods:	
All-purpose flour	6 months
Whole wheat flour	2 to 3 months
Semolina flour	12 months
Cornstarch	12 months
Cornmeal	12 months
Rolled oats	1 month
Salt	6 months
Spices	6 months
Dried herbs	6 months
Baking powder	2 to 3 months
Baking soda	2 to 3 months
Cream of tartar	2 to 3 months
Granulated sugar	12 months
Brown sugar	1 month
Icing sugar	1 month
Dried yeast	6 months
Dried fruit	2 to 3 months
Nuts	1 month
Shredded coconut	1 month
Miscellaneous:	
Pickles	12 months
Jam	12 months
Honey	6 months
Chocolate	1 month
Vanilla extract, etc.	12 months
Food coloring	12 months
Corn syrup	12 months

Milk	4 to 7 days
Cream	3 to 4 days
Butter	2 to 4 weeks
Cheese	1 to 2 weeks
Cream cheese	5 to 7 days
Whole eggs	2 to 3 weeks

FREEZING YOUR ASSETS

Most home-bakes store well in airtight containers or in cookie jars for a week or more, but if you're making a double batch of cookies or a couple of quick breads, why not freeze the extras to enjoy at a later date. The next best thing to baked goodies straight from the oven are those that are quick-frozen after baking. Once thawed, they have that just-made flavor. Breads and rolls keep especially well in the freezer and can be thawed and heated in next to no time.

Pack breads, rolls, cakes, muffins and tea biscuits in freezer bags before storing in the freezer. Store cookies in rigid containers to prevent breakage. Don't forget to label them with the date.

Cakes are best frozen unfrosted although they can, if necessary, be frozen after frosting. Freeze frosted cakes *before* packing in freezer bags and unwrap *before* thawing. Cream filled cakes and pastries don't freeze well.

Here's a quick guide to help you get the best out of baking day.

Home-Bake	Storage Time	How To Thaw
Cookies	6 months	Both baked and unbaked cookies can be frozen, but only Icebox Cookies can be baked from frozen. Thaw the others before baking.
Cakes:		
Unfrosted	6 months	Thaw in freezer bag.
Frosted	2 months	Unwrap before thawing.
Tea Biscuits and Quick Breads	6 months	Thaw in freezer bag, then heat through slightly in a 300°F (150°C) oven.
Muffins	3 months	Same as tea biscuits.
Breads & Rolls	1 month	Thaw in freezer bag. Rolls can be semi-baked (until they start to brown) before freezing. Heat in oven, to thaw and finish cooking.
Fruit Pies	6 months	Can be frozen raw or cooked. Thaw as follows: Raw: bake straight from freezer in a 425°F (220°C) oven for 45 to 55 minutes; Cooked: reheat straight from freezer in a 350°F (180°C) oven for 45 minutes.
Pie Shells:		
Baked	6 months	Thaw in freezer bag, then add filling.
Unbaked	3 months	Bake straight from freezer in a 450°F (230°C) oven for 10 to 15 minutes.
Pastry	3 months	It's useful to roll pastry out to even-sized sheets. Stack them, interleaved with waxed paper, and pack in freezer bags. Can be thawed one at a time when needed.

FIRST AID

Your best defence against the odd disaster that may occur on baking day is a sense of humor. By disasters, I don't mean the distinctly un-funny variety such as severe burns or setting fire to the house—there are people far better qualified than I to write about these. The First Aid that interests me is the kind required when what you remove from the oven doesn't look quite the same as the appetizing photo in the cookbook. Maybe your oven is too hot, or you added too much flour, or the mixture wasn't kneaded enough. Whatever the reason, we're only human and even the most practised bakers occasionally produce less than perfect results.

Of course, laughing off a sunken sponge cake or cookies that are shaped like ink blots is easy in the bosom of one's family, but why is it that the hand of doom always falls on us poor, unsuspecting home-bakers just before that SPECIAL occasion? You know the feeling—it's probably all too familiar.

His boss is coming for dinner and your soon-to-be gâteau is stubbornly lurking in the bottom of the cake pan, refusing to rise. Your mother-in-law is dropping by for coffee and those "oh, so simple to bake" tea biscuits are doing a good impression of chunks of concrete. What do you do, apart from panic?

Unfortunately, some crises are irreversible and you must give those smoldering embers that had promised to stock the cookie jar, a decent burial in the garbage can. Most disasters aren't so disastrous, you'll be happy to learn, and the results can be transformed miraculously at a moment's notice into a dish no one will suspect was a mistake. At worst, you can salvage the remnants of the original and store them for use in some more mundane manner (cake or cookie crumbs can be sprinkled on stewed fruit or canned pie filling for a speedy topping).

Read on and you're sure to find some familiar disasters, together with advice on what went wrong, how to prevent it from happening again and, best of all, what to do with the mess you're left with.

COOKIES

Crisis	Why It Happened To You	What To Do About It
Difficult to roll	If dough was chilled, it may be too hard.	Leave at room temperature for 20 to 30 minutes.
	If sticking to rolling pin, too much butter in mixture. If too crumbly, not enough butter or liquid in mixture.	Try chilling rolling pin. If that doesn't work, form dough into small balls or simply press into an oblong pan and call it shortbread.
Misshapen	Dough too soft or cookie sheet too warm when cookies were first arranged on it.	They'll taste fine, but if you're really consumed by embarrassment, make Gooey Cookie Pud (recipe, p. 29).
Tough	Dough handled too much or trimmings re-rolled. Too much flour used when rolling out or too much liquid in dough.	Treat cookie dough gently before baking. Flour rolling pin and work surface *very* lightly. If using a cookie cutter, cut rounds very close together and discard trimmings. Process tough baked cookies in food processor to make crumbs and use to make cookie crumb crusts for cheese-cakes or sprinkle on desserts for a crunchy topping.
Overcooked	Oven temperature too high, cookies too near sides of cookie sheet or cookie sheet too near top of oven.	Always use a timer when baking cookies and check after minimum baking time specified in recipe. Keep an eye on cookies all the time, especially dark-colored ones that can overcook without you realizing it. It's a good idea to have your oven temperature tested from time to time to ensure its accuracy. Trim burnt bits from cookies and feed remaining parts to kids or make Gooey Cookie Pud (recipe, p. 29).

CAKES

Crisis	Why It Happened To You	What To Do About It
Heavy, unrisen	Not enough raising agent. Fat, sugar, eggs not beaten enough and/or flour folded in too vigorously. In case of chiffon or angel cakes, egg whites not beaten enough and/or folded in too vigorously.	If cake is still edible but unsightly, sprinkle generously with brandy, liqueur or fruit juice and disguise with whipped cream and fruit or chocolate. Or make Trifle (recipe, p. 29). If cake is *really* heavy, try processing into crumbs, then toast and use for cookie crumbs (see above).
Risen very high and cracked on surface	Oven too hot.	Simply slice off cracked top and disguise with frosting or whipped cream.
Bland, ''flat'' tasting	You probably forgot the salt — just a pinch makes all the difference.	Add more flavor by sprinkling generously with brandy or sherry, then call it a dessert and serve with cream.
Cooled cake shrinks dramatically	Cake cooled in a draft. Avoidance next time is too obvious to mention!	Employ same remedies as for heavy, unrisen cakes.
Overcooked	Oven too hot or cake left in oven too long.	Slice off burnt bits and disguise cake with frosting or whipped cream. This only works, of course, if the cake is not actually smoldering!
Cake sinks suddenly when taken from oven.	Did you test the cake with a skewer or cake tester? If so, be a little more gentle with skewer next time.	Poking a cake with a skewer to see if it comes out clean is a good test of doneness but also releases some of the precious air trapped inside the cake which makes it light. Use this test only when you're not sure cake is done — if cake shrinks from sides of pan and top springs back when pressed gently, you can be pretty sure the cake is ready.

JELLY ROLL

Crisis	Why It Happened To You	What To Do About It
Bakes unevenly	The oven shelf, or possibly the whole oven, is on a slant, or the jelly roll pan is warped.	Don't panic! When you roll up the jelly roll, ensure the thinner end is inside.

Crisis	Why It Happened To You	What To Do About It
Sticks to tea towel	Tea towel not sugared enough.	The jelly roll, by the law of averages, is bound to fall apart. If just one end disintegrates, try to roll the jelly roll with this end inside. In the event of the whole thing breaking up, roll it as best you can and disguise with whipped cream. Or abandon the jelly roll idea altogether and call it a Trifle (recipe, p. 29).

MERINGUES

Soggy	Weren't left in oven long enough after baking to dry out.	If there's time, just return to very low oven (250°F/120°C) until "un-sogged". If there's no time, try and scoop out the soggy bits.
Broken	Were dried out too much. Or, you forgot to line the cookie sheet with waxed paper, didn't you?	Make a wonderful dessert by folding the broken meringues into whipped cream (laced with your favorite liqueur, if you like). Serve with strawberries or other fresh fruit.

QUICK BREADS & MUFFINS

Tough	Uncooked batter was overmixed. Batter should be lumpy — a few flecks of flour don't matter.	Sweet quick breads and muffins can be crumbled into a pie dish and sprinkled with fruit juice (or something a little stronger!). Top with fruit, then uncooked meringue, and bake in a 375°F (190°C) oven for 15 to 20 minutes.

TEA BISCUITS

Unrisen	Not enough raising agent. Or tea biscuits not touching each other and sides of pan.	Savory Biscuits: Make mini-pizzas by cutting in half and topping each with tomato paste, olives, mushrooms and grated cheese, and broiling until topping bubbles. Or, crumble over cooked casserole or stew, top with grated cheese and broil. Sweet Biscuits: Crumble over hot stewed fruit or canned pie filling, sprinkle with brown sugar and broil.

Crisis	Why It Happened To You	What To Do About It
Tough and Chewy	Dough too wet or handled too much before baking.	Remedies same as for unrisen tea biscuits.

FRUIT BREAD & CAKES

Fruit sinks to bottom	Cake batter too runny or cake pan knocked by accident before it went into oven.	If it's *really* sunk, slice cake in half horizontally and treat as two separate cakes. Top fruitless half with frosting or whipped cream and serve fruit-full half heated through in oven and topped with custard sauce or cream. To avoid fruit sinking *next* time, reserve one-quarter of specified amount of flour and toss fruit in this before adding to cake batter.

PASTRY

Soggy	Oven not hot enough or uncooked pastry too warm.	Unfortunately, pastry is one of those things that are difficult to salvage. Next time, follow these two rules: • Pastry dough must be kept as cold as possible. • Handle the dough as little as possible.
Tough	Fat too rich — a combination of butter and shortening is best. Water too warm. Too much flour used when rolling. Or dough too warm or handled too much.	See above.

EMERGENCY SUPPLIES

If you keep certain items in your cupboard, refrigerator or freezer, you'll be ready for any crisis that baking day may throw at you.

In the cupboard:	• good quality jams
	• canned fruit (cherries and mandarin oranges are especially useful)
	• assorted nuts
	• semi-sweet chocolate
	• icing sugar
	• assorted cake decorations
	• glacé cherries
	• brandy and/or sherry
	• liqueur(s)
	• fruit juice
	• variety of spices
	• pudding mixes
	• custard powder

In the refrigerator:	• whipping cream (or can of aerosol whipped cream)
	• sour cream
	• eggs
	• butter
	• fresh fruit (lemons, oranges and kiwi fruit are handy)
	• Cheddar cheese

These two emergency recipes have saved a few disasters for me. Quantities are unimportant as they depend on the size of the crisis and the number of people you're trying to fool (I mean, feed!). Anyway, who has time to measure things in a real crisis?

Gooey Cookie Pud

Break up cookies and layer in serving bowl with whipped cream and a sharp fruit, such as drained, canned mandarin oranges. Finish with a layer of whipped cream. If the cookies are fairly plain, sprinkling the cookies with a little spice, such as nutmeg or ginger, adds zip. This is best chilled overnight but at a pinch can be served after an hour or so.

Trifle

This wonderful dessert never fails to impress. I've even been known to make it on purpose—rather than by accident. Split your disastrous sponge cake in half horizontally and sandwich the two halves together with jam. Cut into small pieces and place in a serving bowl. Sprinkle with brandy, sherry or (for younger guests) fruit juice. Top with fresh or canned fruit. Cover completely with thick custard (either "proper", home-made egg custard, or use the "instant" kind). Leave to set, preferably overnight. Shortly before serving, cover custard with whipped cream and decorate tastefully. Some winning combinations of ingredients include: chocolate cake, canned black cherries and kirsch; vanilla sponge, canned apricots and brandy; almond sponge, strawberries and sherry.

Pinwheel Icebox Cookies

2

CALLING ALL COOKIE MONSTERS

When it comes to filling the cookie jar, we're really talking quick 'n' easy. None of these recipes will take much more than 20 minutes of your time and most whisk in and out of the oven in under 15. Even confirmed non-bakers will find it difficult to go back to store-bought cookies after tasting the good old-fashioned flavor of home-bakes. In fact, cookie and bar recipes, with their uncomplicated methods and easy cleanup, are ideal for novice bakers to cut their teeth on (excuse the pun!).

There are cookies and bars here for everyone: chocoholics, nut nuts, crisp cookie addicts, and those who like something to chew on. From homey crunchy bars for the lunch pail, to delicious dunkable cookies for the midnight hour, your cookie jar will cater to any occasion. There are even a couple of posh, but embarrassingly easy, recipes to serve when you're out to impress, that you positively wouldn't dream of dunking!

CHERRY FINGERS

Preparation Time
10 minutes
Cooking Time
35 minutes
Makes
12 fingers

Using both red and green glacé cherries makes these fruity fingers extra colorful. The rich, crumbly dough is best when made with butter; you can use margarine but the flavor won't be as good.

1-1/3 cups	all-purpose flour	325 mL
2 tbsp	cornstarch	25 mL
1/2 cup	butter	125 mL
1/4 cup	vanilla sugar (see Quick Tip, p. 32) or granulated sugar	50 mL
1 cup	glacé cherries, chopped	250 mL

1 Preheat oven to 325°F (160°C). Have ready a shallow nonstick or lightly greased 11- × 7-inch (28 × 18 cm) cake pan.

2 In a medium bowl, sift together flour and cornstarch. With your fingertips or pastry blender, rub in butter until mixture resembles fine crumbs. Stir in sugar.

3 Spoon half the mixture into cake pan. With palms of your hands, press over base of pan. Scatter chopped cherries evenly over top, then sprinkle with remaining flour mixture. Press down lightly with your hands.

4 Bake for 35 minutes or until golden and firm. Cut into bars while still warm and let cool in pan.

QUICK TIP

Vanilla Sugar is easy to make and can be used to add delicate vanilla flavor to many different baking and dessert recipes. Substitute Vanilla Sugar in recipes which call for granulated sugar and vanilla extract. Simply fill a medium-sized preserving jar almost to the top with granulated sugar and bury a couple of vanilla beans in the center. Screw the lid on firmly and leave for about a week before using, shaking occasionally. Every time you use some sugar from the jar, top it up with more granulated sugar and you'll have a constant supply of Vanilla Sugar. The sugar and vanilla beans will keep indefinitely.

GINGER NUTS

Preparation Time
20 minutes
Cooking Time
10 to 12 minutes
Makes
12 to 15 ginger nuts

Ginger, with its fresh, lemony flavor, is one of my favorite spices. These chewy cookies pack a double helping of ginger — both ground and preserved — although you won't find the spice overpowering. All you dunkers will be pleased to hear that this is the quintessential dunking cookie. It's heavenly with ice-cold milk!

1/2 cup	shortening	125 mL
1/3 cup	firmly packed brown sugar	75 mL
1/3 cup	corn syrup	75 mL
1-1/3 cups	all-purpose flour	325 mL
1-1/2 tsp	ground ginger	7 mL
1/2 tsp	baking powder	2 mL
Pinch	salt	Pinch
1/2 tsp	baking soda	2 mL
1-1/2 tsp	milk	7 mL
1/4 cup	finely chopped preserved ginger	50 mL

1 Preheat oven to 350°F (180°C). Have ready two nonstick or lightly greased cookie sheets.

2 In a medium saucepan over low heat, heat together shortening, sugar and syrup, stirring occasionally, until shortening has melted.

3 Meanwhile, in a medium bowl, sift together flour, ground ginger, baking powder and salt. In a small cup, dissolve baking soda in milk.

4 When shortening has melted, remove saucepan from heat and add flour mixture. Stir to blend well and form a thick paste. Add milk mixture and mix well. Stir in preserved ginger.

5 With dampened hands, form mixture into 12 to 15 walnut-sized balls. Place, about 3 inches (8 cm) apart, on cookie sheets and flatten slightly with blade of a knife. Bake for 10 to 12 minutes or until golden brown. Leave on cookie sheets for 2 minutes to firm up, then transfer to a wire rack and let cool completely.

THE DEFINITIVE CHOCOLATE CHUNK COOKIE

Preparation Time
15 minutes
Cooking Time
10 to 12 minutes
Makes
18 to 20 cookies

These could be subtitled "Please Yourself Cookies" because you can add all sorts of different ingredients to vary the flavor. Instead of granola, try rolled oats or chopped nuts (almonds and pecans are especially good), or add 1/2 cup (125 mL) sultana raisins instead of coconut. Of course, there's no substitute for oodles of chocolate chunks!

1/2 cup	butter or margarine (at room temperature)	125 mL
1/3 cup	granulated sugar	75 mL
1/4 cup	firmly packed brown sugar	50 mL
1	large egg	1
1/2 tsp	almond extract	2 mL
1-1/3 cups	all-purpose flour	325 mL
1/2 tsp	baking soda	2 mL
1/2 tsp	salt	2 mL
4 oz	semi-sweet chocolate (see Quick Tip, p. 141).	125 g
1/2 cup	granola with honey and almonds	125 mL
1/2 cup	unsweetened shredded coconut	125 mL

1 Preheat oven to 375°F (190°C). Have ready two nonstick or lightly greased cookie sheets.

2 In a medium bowl, beat together butter and both sugars until pale beige and fluffy. Beat in egg and almond extract.

3 In a separate bowl, sift together flour, baking soda and salt. Gradually stir flour mixture into butter mixture until smooth.

4 Chop chocolate roughly into 1/4- to 1/2-inch (5 mm to 1 cm) chunks. Add to cookie dough along with granola and coconut and work in with your hands until ingredients are well combined.

5 Drop tablespoonfuls of the mixture, about 2 inches (5 cm) apart, onto cookie sheets. Bake for 10 to 12 minutes until lightly browned. Leave on cookie sheets for 2 minutes to firm up, then transfer to a wire rack and let cool completely.

QUICK TIP

For best results, always use the type of chocolate that's called for in a recipe, and make sure it really *is* pure chocolate you're buying. There are many products available containing chocolate *flavoring* which just don't give the same results as the real thing!

ROCK CAKES

Preparation Time
10 minutes
Cooking Time
15 minutes
Makes
about 10 rock cakes

These rough, uneven-looking cookies must have earned their name from their appearance because biting into one of these light, spicy morsels will certainly not leave you instantly toothless!

2 cups	all-purpose flour	500 mL
1 tsp	baking powder	5 mL
1/2 tsp	ground allspice	2 mL
Pinch	salt	Pinch
3/4 cup	butter or margarine	175 mL
3/4 cup	sultana raisins	175 mL
1/2 cup	granulated sugar	125 mL
1	large egg, beaten	1
1/3 cup	milk (approx)	75 mL

1 Preheat oven to 400°F (200°C). Have ready two nonstick or lightly greased cookie sheets.

2 In a medium bowl, sift together flour, baking powder, allspice and salt. With your fingertips or pastry blender, rub in butter until mixture resembles fine crumbs. Stir in sultanas and sugar. Add egg, then stir in milk, a little at a time, until mixture is a soft, dropping consistency.

3 Drop tablespoonfuls of the mixture, about 2 inches (5 cm) apart, onto cookie sheets. Bake for 15 minutes or until golden brown. Transfer to wire rack and let cool.

PEANUT BARS

Preparation Time
10 minutes
Cooking Time
10 to 12 minutes
Makes
about 15 bars

Luckily these Peanut Bars are quick to make because, whether you tuck a couple into the kids' lunch pails or serve them up at snack time, they'll disappear in minutes.

1/2 cup	butter or margarine (at room temperature)	125 mL
1/2 cup	firmly packed brown sugar	125 mL
1/2 cup	crunchy peanut butter	125 mL
1-1/3 cups	all-purpose flour	325 mL
1/4 cup	chopped salted peanuts (optional)	50 mL

1 Preheat oven to 350°F (180°C). Have ready two nonstick or lightly greased cookie sheets.

2 In a medium bowl, beat together butter and sugar until pale beige and fluffy. Beat in peanut butter, then flour, until ingredients are well combined. Knead mixture for about 2 minutes or until it holds together, then turn out onto a lightly floured surface.

3 Roll out dough to 1/4 inch (5 mm) thickness. The mixture will be quite crumbly so you may need to press it together as you roll. Trim the edges as square as possible. Scatter chopped peanuts, if used, over dough and roll lightly with rolling pin to press in. Cut dough into about 15 bars and place, about 2 inches (5 cm) apart, on cookie sheets. Bake for 10 to 12 minutes until golden brown. Leave on cookie sheets for 2 minutes to firm up, then transfer to wire rack and let cool completely.

CHOCOLATE STUFF

don't like

Preparation Time
20 minutes
Cooking Time
25 minutes
Makes
8 bars

A wonderful cook, although not too imaginative at naming recipes, my mother invented these rich, chocolaty bars years ago. They have been a family favorite ever since.

3/4 cup	butter or margarine	175 mL
1 cup	all-purpose flour	250 mL
2 tbsp	unsweetened cocoa powder	25 mL
1 tsp	baking powder	5 mL
1 cup	unsweetened shredded coconut	250 mL
1 cup	cornflakes	250 mL
2/3 cup	granulated sugar	150 mL
4 oz	semi-sweet chocolate (see Quick Tip, p. 141)	125 g
1 tbsp	vegetable oil	15 mL

1 Preheat oven to 350°F (180°C). Have ready a shallow, nonstick or lightly greased 8-inch (20 cm) square cake pan.

2 In a medium saucepan over low heat, melt butter. Meanwhile, in a medium bowl, sift together flour, cocoa and baking powder.

3 When butter has melted, remove saucepan from heat and add coconut, cornflakes, sugar and flour mixture. Stir until ingredients are well combined. Evenly spread mixture in cake pan. Bake for 25 minutes or until firm to the touch. Score into 8 bars while still warm and let cool in cake pan.

4 In a small bowl over a saucepan of gently simmering water, or in top of double boiler, melt chocolate with vegetable oil, stirring occasionally until smooth. Pour over Chocolate Stuff and spread with back of a spoon. Let set, then cut into bars.

LEMON AND CARDAMOM FILIGREE COOKIES

Preparation Time
10 minutes
Cooking Time
10 minutes
Makes
about 18 cookies

These delicate cookies spread to a lacy thinness, making them an ideal treat to serve with after-dinner coffee or as an accompaniment to ice cream.

1/2 cup	butter or margarine (at room temperature)	125 mL
2/3 cup	firmly packed brown sugar	150 mL
1/4 cup	all-purpose flour	50 mL
1 tsp	ground cardamom	5 mL
1	lemon, grated rind	1
2 tbsp	milk	25 mL
1-1/3 cups	rolled oats	325 mL

1 Preheat oven to 350°F (180°C). Have ready two nonstick or lightly greased cookie sheets.

2 In a medium bowl, beat together butter and sugar until pale beige and fluffy.

3 In a separate bowl, sift together flour and cardamom. Fold into creamed mixture along with lemon rind. Add milk and oats and work mixture with your hands until ingredients are well combined.

4 Drop teaspoonfuls of the mixture, about 3 inches (8 cm) apart, onto the cookie sheets. Bake for 10 minutes until golden brown and lacy-looking. Leave on cookie sheets for 5 minutes to firm up, then very carefully transfer to wire rack and let cool completely.

ORANGE AND WALNUT MACAROONS

Preparation Time
15 minutes

Cooking Time
20 minutes

Makes
8 to 10 macaroons

Nut nuts will love these delicate cookies, rich in walnuts and tangy with orange. Stiffly whisked egg whites give the cookies a light, chewy texture.

1/2 cup	chopped walnuts	125 mL
2/3 cup	granulated sugar	150 mL
1/2 cup	semolina flour	125 mL
1	orange, grated rind	1
2	large egg whites (see Quick Tip, p. 39)	2
2 tbsp	chopped walnuts for decoration	25 mL

1 Preheat oven to 350°F (180°C). Have ready two nonstick or baking parchment-lined cookie sheets.

2 In a coffee grinder or food processor fitted with a metal blade, process 1/2 cup (125 mL) chopped walnuts until finely ground. Transfer ground nuts to medium bowl and mix together with sugar, flour and orange rind.

3 In a separate bowl, whisk egg whites with wire whisk or an electric mixer until they stand in stiff peaks. With a metal spoon, gradually fold dry ingredients into whisked egg whites until ingredients are well combined.

4 Drop tablespoonfuls of the mixture, about 3 inches (8 cm) apart, onto cookie sheets. Place a few pieces of chopped walnuts on top of each. Bake for 20 minutes or until golden brown and firm. Leave on cookie sheets for 2 minutes to firm up, then carefully transfer to wire rack and let cool completely.

QUICK TIP

For the lightest, fluffiest whisked egg whites, eggs should be at room temperature. When making meringues or macaroons, take eggs from the refrigerator an hour or so ahead of time. Make sure, too, that your bowl and whisk are completely clean and grease-free.

ICEBOX COOKIES

The speediest and most convenient of cookies, these will store well in your refrigerator or freezer until you're ready to bake. Simply slice as many cookies as you need from the roll of dough and in minutes you'll have a plateful of crisp, buttery home-bakes.

All kinds of extra ingredients and flavorings can be added to the basic recipe with the variations as endless as your imagination allows. I've included my three favorites here. Try them and then experiment to create your very own icebox cookie.

BASIC ICEBOX COOKIES

Preparation Time
10 minutes
(excluding chilling)

Cooking Time
10 to 15 minutes

Makes
about 20 cookies

1-1/2 cups	all-purpose flour	375 mL
1 tsp	baking powder	5 mL
1/2 tsp	salt	2 mL
1/2 cup	butter or margarine (at room temperature)	125 mL
2/3 cup	granulated sugar	150 mL
1	large egg	1

1 In a medium bowl, sift together flour, baking powder and salt. In a separate bowl, beat together butter, sugar and egg until pale yellow and fluffy. Add dry ingredients to butter mixture and work together with your hands until ingredients are well combined.

2 Turn out dough onto an unfloured surface and form into a roll about 1-1/2 inches (3.5 cm) in diameter (a few lumps and bumps don't matter). Wrap roll in plastic wrap or aluminum foil and chill in refrigerator for at least 3 hours before baking.

3 Roll of dough will keep for up to 2 weeks in the refrigerator or can be frozen for up to 6 months. Allow frozen dough to thaw slightly before slicing and increase baking time by 2 to 3 minutes.

4 When ready to cook, heat oven to 375°F (190°C) and have a cookie sheet ready. Unwrap dough and, using a very sharp knife and with a sawing motion, slice as many 1/8- to 1/4-inch (3 to 5 mm) thick cookies as you wish. Place, about 2 inches (5 cm) apart, on cookie sheet and bake for 10 to 15 minutes or until light golden. Transfer to wire rack and let cool.

VARIATIONS

FRUIT 'N' SPICE ICEBOX COOKIES

Preparation Time
15 minutes
(excluding chilling)

Before forming Basic Icebox Cookie dough (see p. 40) into a roll, knead in 1/4 cup (50 mL) currants, 1/4 cup (50 mL) peel, 1/4 tsp (1 mL) nutmeg, and 1/4 tsp (1 mL) cinnamon, until ingredients are well combined. Form into a roll, wrap, chill and bake as described in Basic Icebox Cookie recipe.

ALMOND ORANGE ICEBOX COOKIES

Preparation Time
15 minutes
(excluding chilling)

Before forming Basic Icebox Cookie dough (see p. 40) into a roll, knead in 1 tsp (5 mL) almond extract and grated rind from 1 orange until ingredients are well combined. Form into a roll, wrap, chill and bake as described in the Basic Icebox Cookie recipe.

CHOCOLATE MINT PINWHEEL ICEBOX COOKIES

Preparation Time
25 minutes

Cooking Time
10 to 15 minutes

Makes
about 20 cookies

This version of icebox cookies takes a little longer to prepare and is a little trickier, but your efforts will be well rewarded when you take the pretty green and brown cookies from the oven.

	Basic Icebox Cookie dough (see p. 40)	
1/4 tsp	peppermint extract	1 mL
	Few drops green food coloring	
1 oz	semi-sweet chocolate (see Quick Tip, p. 141)	30 g
	Icing sugar	

1 Divide Basic Icebox Cookie dough in half and put in separate bowls. Into one half, knead in peppermint extract and enough food coloring to tint dough pale green.

2 Meanwhile, in a small bowl over a saucepan of gently simmering water or in top of double boiler, melt chocolate, stirring occasionally until smooth. Add chocolate to other half of dough and knead in until evenly distributed.

3 Dust two 18- × 12-inch (46 × 30 cm) sheets of waxed paper with sugar. Place portion of dough on each sheet. Using a rolling pin dusted with more sugar, roll out dough into 11- × 8-inch (27 × 20 cm) rectangles. It's unlikely to be exact, but as long as both rectangles of dough are about the same size, actual dimensions aren't too important.

4 Using the paper to lift dough, carefully invert chocolate portion on top of peppermint, lining up edges. Peel away top piece of paper. Trim edges as evenly as possible, then, starting at one of the long sides, carefully roll up like a jelly roll, peeling paper away as you go.

5 Wrap in plastic wrap or aluminum foil, chill and bake as described in the Basic Icebox Cookie recipe.

Italian Pizza Tea Bread

3

BREADS IN BRIEF

I chose the title for this section, not because I could only come up with a couple of recipes, but because bread-making can be much speedier than you'd imagine.

This is my favorite type of baking. Quick breads and tea breads, raised with soda or baking powder instead of time-consuming yeast, whip up in next to no time. The results may not have the same "light-as-air" texture as yeast-risen breads but they come a very wholesome second and are just as versatile.

As you'd expect, there are some deliciously rich fruit-filled tea breads, plus some unusual savory versions. There's good old-fashioned soda bread, and—everyone's favorite—moist, light tea biscuits.

With the exceptions of soda bread and tea biscuits, which are best eaten the day they're baked (although soda bread is tasty after a day or two if toasted or heated through), the other breads in this section are good keepers if stored in airtight containers. Some, such as Rich Fruit Loaf, actually improve with keeping. Mind you, once your kitchen is filled with that lovely warm aroma that tells everyone it's baking day, and the breads come steaming from the oven, there'll be little left to store but crumbs!

TROPICAL TEA BREAD

Preparation Time
15 minutes
Cooking Time
1 hour
Makes
1 loaf

As its name suggests, this tea bread contains all kinds of exotica, although the ingredients are probably already in your cupboard: canned pineapple, dried apricots and shredded coconut.

1/2 cup	butter or margarine (at room temperature)	125 mL
1/2 cup	firmly packed brown sugar	125 mL
1	large egg	1
1 cup	chopped dried apricots (see Quick Tip, p. 46)	250 mL
1 cup	canned crushed pineapple (drained)	250 mL
1 tsp	baking soda dissolved in 1 tbsp (15 mL) water	5 mL
1-1/2 cups	all-purpose flour	375 mL
1 tsp	baking powder	5 mL
1 tbsp	unsweetened shredded coconut	15 mL

1 Preheat oven to 325°F (160°C). Have ready a nonstick or lightly greased 8-1/2- × 4-1/2-inch (6 cup/1.5 L) loaf pan.

2 In a medium bowl, beat together butter, sugar and egg until pale beige and fluffy. Stir in apricots, pineapple and dissolved baking soda.

3 In a separate bowl, sift together flour and baking powder. With a fork, gradually stir dry ingredients into fruit mixture until well combined.

4 Spoon into loaf pan and smooth surface. Sprinkle coconut evenly over top. Bake for 1 hour or until risen and golden brown, and skewer inserted in center comes out clean. Turn out and let cool on a wire rack.

QUICK TIP

Chop dried fruits, such as apricots and dates, quickly and easily by snipping them with kitchen scissors rather than cutting them with a knife.

CRUNCHY ZUCCHINI LOAF

Preparation Time
15 minutes
Cooking Time
1 hour
Makes
1 loaf

Peanut butter fans will enjoy this loaf, sliced and topped with their favorite nutty spread. Everyone else will be content with butter, but all will appreciate its crumbly, crunchy texture and nutty taste.

2 cups	all-purpose flour	500 mL
1 tbsp	baking powder	15 mL
1/2 tsp	salt	2 mL
1/3 cup	crunchy peanut butter	75 mL
3 tbsp	butter or margarine	45 mL
1	large zucchini, trimmed and grated	1
2	large eggs, beaten	2
1/3 cup	milk (plus a little extra, if necessary)	75 mL

1 Preheat oven to 350°F (180°C). Have ready a nonstick or lightly greased 8-1/2- × 4-1/2-inch (6 cup/1.5 L) loaf pan.

2 In a medium bowl, sift together flour, baking powder and salt. With your fingertips or pastry blender, rub in peanut butter and butter until mixture resembles fine crumbs. Add zucchini and stir well.

3 Add eggs and milk. With a fork, mix until well combined and stiff dough is formed.

4 Spoon into loaf pan and smooth surface. Bake for 1 hour or until risen and golden, and skewer inserted in center comes out clean. Turn out and let cool on a wire rack.

RICH FRUIT LOAF

Preparation Time
15 minutes
(excluding soaking time)
Cooking Time
50 minutes
to 1 hour
Makes
1 loaf

Vary the flavorings of this fruit-filled loaf: add grated lemon rind, your favorite spices, or a dollop of marmalade to the ingredients, or substitute some dried apricots or dates for the sultanas and currants. This loaf keeps very well in an airtight tin.

1-3/4 cups	mixed dried fruit (sultanas, currants, etc.)	425 mL
1/2 cup	firmly packed brown sugar	125 mL
2/3 cup	hot black tea	150 mL
2 cups	all-purpose flour	500 mL
1 tbsp	baking powder	15 mL
1/2 tsp	ground allspice	2 mL
1	orange	1
1	large egg, beaten	1

1 Measure fruit and sugar into a medium bowl and pour hot tea over mixture. Stir well and set aside to soak for at least 3 hours (preferably overnight).

2 After fruit has soaked, preheat oven to 350°F (180°C). Have ready a nonstick or lightly greased 8-1/2- × 4-1/2-inch (6 cup/1.5 L) loaf pan.

3 In a large bowl, sift together flour, baking powder and allspice. Grate rind from orange and stir into flour mixture. Add fruit mixture, squeezed juice from orange, and egg. Mix until well combined.

4 Spoon into loaf pan and smooth surface. Bake for 50 minutes to 1 hour or until risen and golden brown, and skewer inserted in center comes out clean. Check the loaf after 30 minutes and cover with a piece of aluminum foil if top is browning too much. Turn out and let cool on a wire rack.

ITALIAN PIZZA TEA BREAD

Preparation Time
15 minutes
Cooking Time
40 minutes
Makes
1 loaf

Moist and herby, this recipe takes the traditional pizza flavors of cheese, basil and tomatoes and turns them into a delicious savory tea bread. It makes a great snack served sliced, topped with cheese, and popped under the broiler until bubbling.

2 cups	all-purpose flour	500 mL
1 tbsp	baking powder	15 mL
1/2 tsp	salt	2 mL
3 tbsp	butter or margarine	45 mL
1/3 cup	grated Parmesan cheese	75 mL
2 tsp	dried basil	10 mL
2	large eggs, beaten	2
2/3 cup	tomato juice	150 mL

1 Preheat oven to 375°F (190°C). Have ready a nonstick or lightly greased 8-1/2- × 4-1/2-inch (6 cup/1.5 L) loaf pan.

2 In a medium bowl, sift together flour, baking powder and salt. With your fingertips or pastry blender, rub in butter until mixture resembles fine crumbs. Stir in cheese and basil. Add eggs and tomato juice. With a fork, mix until well combined and stiff dough is formed. Spoon into loaf pan and smooth surface level. Bake for 40 minutes or until risen and golden brown, and skewer inserted in center comes out clean. Turn out and let cool on a wire rack.

BANANA LOAF

Preparation Time
15 minutes
Cooking Time
1 hour
Makes
1 loaf

Many thanks to Linda Fisher, my loyal typist and good friend, for this beautifully moist tea bread. Served warm from the oven, it literally melts in your mouth but is equally good served cold, sliced and buttered.

1/2 cup	butter or margarine (at room temperature)	125 mL
2/3 cup	granulated sugar	150 mL
1	large egg	1
2	large ripe bananas, peeled and mashed	2
1 tsp	baking soda dissolved in 1 tbsp (15 mL) water	5 mL
1-1/2 cups	all-purpose flour	375 mL
1 tsp	baking powder	5 mL
1 tbsp	chopped walnuts (optional)	15 mL

1 Preheat oven to 325°F (160°C). Have ready a nonstick or lightly greased 8-1/2- × 4-1/2-inch (6 cup/1.5 L) loaf pan.

2 In a medium bowl, beat together butter, sugar and egg until pale yellow and fluffy. Beat in bananas and dissolved baking soda until well combined. The mixture may look slightly curdled at this point.

3 In a separate bowl, sift together flour and baking powder. Gradually fold flour into banana mixture until well combined.

4 Spoon into loaf pan and smooth surface. Sprinkle chopped walnuts over top, if used, and bake for 1 hour or until risen and golden, and cake tester inserted in center comes out clean. Turn out and let cool on a wire rack.

TRADITIONAL SODA BREAD

Preparation Time
10 minutes
Cooking Time
25 to 30 minutes
Makes
1 loaf

Most yeast-raised breads take quite a while to prepare so, for a speedy substitute, this moist bread raised with baking soda is hard to beat. A firm favorite in its native Ireland, it's best served warm from the oven with loads of butter (see Quick Tip, p. 51).

3 cups	all-purpose flour	750 mL
1 tbsp	baking powder	15 mL
1 tsp	baking soda	5 mL
1 tsp	salt	5 mL
3 tbsp	shortening	45 mL
1-1/3 to 1-1/2 cups	milk	325 to 375 mL

1 Preheat oven to 425°F (220°C). Have ready a nonstick or lightly greased cookie sheet.

2 In a medium bowl, sift together flour, baking powder, baking soda and salt. With your fingertips or pastry blender, rub in shortening until mixture resembles fine crumbs. With a fork, gradually mix in enough milk to form a soft but not sticky dough.

3 Turn out dough onto a lightly floured surface and knead lightly for 2 to 3 minutes or until dough is free of cracks. Form into a round about 2 inches (5 cm) thick and place on cookie sheet. With a sharp knife, cut a cross, about 1 inch (2.5 cm) deep, in top of dough. Sprinkle with flour and bake for 25 to 30 minutes or until risen and golden brown, and loaf sounds hollow when tapped on the bottom. Let cool on a wire rack.

QUICK TIP

Soda bread is at its best baked plain and simple and served with lots of butter. If you feel the urge to be creative, however, you can embellish the loaf with different toppings before baking — grated cheese, beaten egg, sesame seeds or warmed honey — or even add extra ingredients to the basic dough — 1 tbsp (15 mL) caraway seeds or 1-1/2 cups (375 mL) mixed dried fruit.

DATE AND GINGER LOAF

Preparation Time
20 minutes
Cooking Time
40 minutes
Makes
1 loaf

A simple, gingery frosting makes this loaf extra special. For a shortcut alternative topping, sprinkle the loaf with 1 tbsp (15 mL) brown sugar before baking.

2 cups	all-purpose flour	500 mL
1 tbsp	baking powder	15 mL
3 tbsp	butter or margarine	45 mL
1/2 cup	firmly packed brown sugar	125 mL
1 cup	chopped pitted dates	250 mL
1/4 cup	finely chopped preserved ginger	50 mL
2	large eggs, beaten	2
2/3 cup	milk	150 mL
Frosting:		
3/4 cup	icing sugar	175 mL
2 tbsp	preserved ginger syrup	25 mL
1 tbsp	water (optional)	15 mL

1 Preheat oven to 375°F (190°C). Have ready a nonstick or lightly greased 8-1/2- × 4-1/2-inch (6 cup/1.5 L) loaf pan.

2 In a medium bowl, sift together flour and baking powder. With your fingertips or pastry blender, rub in butter until mixture resembles fine crumbs. Stir in sugar, dates and ginger.

3 Add eggs and milk. With a fork, mix until well combined and stiff dough is formed. Spoon into loaf pan and smooth surface. Bake for 40 minutes or until risen and golden, and skewer inserted in center comes out clean. Turn out and let cool on a wire rack.

4 *Frosting:* Sift icing sugar into a medium bowl. Stir in ginger syrup. Beat in water, if necessary, to make a smooth, pourable frosting. Place plate under wire rack with cooled loaf. Pour frosting evenly over top of loaf and let set.

CHEESE AND CELERY CORNBREAD

Preparation Time
15 minutes
Cooking Time
25 to 30 minutes
Makes
*one 8-inch (20 cm)
square loaf*

This savory bread is a fine accompaniment to any meal but is especially good with a hearty, rib-sticking soup. If you prefer, you can omit the celery—the bread will be just as delicious.

1/2 cup	shortening	125 mL
3/4 cup	all-purpose flour	175 mL
3/4 cup	cornmeal	175 mL
1 tbsp	baking powder	15 mL
1/2 tsp	salt	2 mL
1/2 tsp	powdered mustard	2 mL
1 cup	grated Cheddar cheese	250 mL
2	stalks celery, finely chopped	2
1	large egg	1
2/3 cup	milk	150 mL

1 In a small saucepan over low heat, melt shortening. Remove from heat and let cool. Preheat oven to 425°F (220°C). Have ready a nonstick or lightly greased 8-inch (20 cm) square cake pan.

2 In a medium bowl, sift together flour, cornmeal, baking powder, salt and mustard. Stir in cheese and celery.

3 In a separate bowl, beat together egg and milk. Add to dry ingredients along with melted shortening and, with a fork, mix just until combined.

4 Spoon into cake pan and smooth surface. Bake for 25 minutes or until risen and golden, and skewer inserted in center comes out clean. Let cool in pan for 5 minutes, then cut into squares. Let cool completely in cake pan.

TEA BISCUITS

Preparation Time
10 minutes
Cooking Time
12 to 15 minutes
Makes
6 to 8 biscuits

Also known as scones, these light little cakes are made from a mixture similar to that used for tea breads and soda bread so they fit quite comfortably into this section.

For the lightest, most delicate tea biscuits, handle the dough as little as possible. After stamping out rounds with the pastry cutter, don't be tempted to re-roll the trimmings and stamp out more rounds as these will be tough and won't rise as well.

The basic tea biscuit dough is extremely versatile. By adding different flavorings, sweet or savory versions can be baked. The unflavored dough can also be rolled out thinly to a large round and used as a speedy pizza base.

Tea biscuits don't store well; they are best eaten the day they're baked — preferably warm from the oven.

2 cups	all-purpose flour	500 mL
1 tbsp	baking powder	15 mL
1/2 tsp	salt	2 mL
1/4 cup	shortening	50 mL
1/4 cup	butter or margarine	50 mL
3/4 cup	milk	175 mL
	Beaten egg for glaze	

1 Preheat oven to 450°F (230°C). Warm a nonstick or lightly greased and floured 8-inch (20 cm) square cake pan.

2 In a medium bowl, sift together flour, baking powder and salt. With your fingertips or pastry blender, rub in shortening and butter until mixture resembles fine crumbs. Gradually add milk to mixture and, with a fork, mix until a soft, but not sticky, dough is formed.

3 Turn out dough onto a lightly floured surface and knead for a few seconds, about 2 to 3 times. Pat into a round about 1/2-inch (1 cm) thick. With a 2-inch (5 cm) floured cookie cutter, cut into rounds, taking care not to twist cutter as you cut.

4 Arrange biscuits in cake pan so they touch each other and sides of the pan. (This stops the biscuits from spreading and makes them rise higher.) Brush tops of biscuits with beaten egg. Bake for 12 to 15 minutes or until risen and golden brown. Remove from cake pan and let cool on a wire rack.

VARIATIONS

LEMON AND CHERRY TEA BISCUITS

Makes *9 biscuits*

These sweet, fruity tea biscuits are delicious served warm or cold and topped with whipped cream and fruit preserves.

Add 2 tbsp (25 mL) granulated sugar and 1/2 cup (125 mL) washed, dried and chopped glacé cherries, to basic tea biscuit mixture before adding milk. Continue as in basic Tea Biscuit recipe (see p. 54).

APPLE, CHEESE AND WALNUT TEA BISCUITS

Makes *9 biscuits*

Serve this sweet/savory variation warm from the oven, spread with lots of butter.

Add 1 apple, peeled, cored and grated; 1 cup (250 mL) grated Cheddar cheese; and 1/2 cup (125 mL) chopped walnuts to basic tea biscuit mixture before adding milk. Continue as in basic Tea Biscuit recipe (see p. 54). Allow 5 minutes extra baking time.

HAM AND MUSTARD TEA BISCUITS

Makes *9 biscuits*

A light and tasty accompaniment to soup or salad.

Add 4 oz (125 g) chopped ham, and 1 tbsp (15 mL) mustard seeds to basic tea biscuit mixture before adding milk. Continue as in basic Tea Biscuit recipe (see p. 54). A little grated Cheddar cheese can be sprinkled on top of biscuits before baking, if desired.

QUICK TIP

Top a casserole with rounds of tea biscuit dough during the last 30 minutes of its cooking time. Increase oven temperature to 400°F (200°C) and, voilà, you have a delicious rich topping. Add 2 tbsp (25 mL) granulated sugar to the basic dough and use these sweet biscuits in the same way to top stewed fruit or canned pie filling.

LEMON AND BLUEBERRY CRUNCH

Preparation Time
25 minutes
Cooking Time
40 to 50 minutes
Makes
one 8-inch (20 cm) round cake

When blueberries are in season, this mouth-watering recipe should be at the top of your list of goodies to make. If you can't wait for midsummer, however, frozen blueberries work just as well. The golden crunchy topping makes this tea-time treat extra special. Cut the round in wedges to serve or break up into individual balls.

3 cups	all-purpose flour	750 mL
2 tsps	baking powder	10 mL
1/2 tsp	salt	2 mL
Pinch	grated nutmeg	Pinch
1	lemon, grated rind	1
1/2 cup	butter or margarine	125 mL
1/2 cup	shortening	125 mL
1/3 cup	granulated sugar	75 mL
2 cups	blueberries, fresh or frozen, thawed and drained	500 mL
2 tsps	baking soda	10 mL
2/3 cup	milk	150 mL
2 tbsp	butter	25 mL
1/4 cup	firmly packed brown sugar	50 mL

1 Preheat oven to 375°F (190°C). Have ready a nonstick or lightly greased 8-inch (20 cm) round cake pan.

2 In a large bowl, sift together flour, baking powder, salt and nutmeg. Stir in lemon rind. With your fingertips or pastry blender, rub in butter and shortening until mixture resembles fine crumbs. Stir in granulated sugar and blueberries until well combined.

3 In a cup, dissolve baking soda in milk, and add to blueberry mixture. With a fork, stir until dough is soft but not sticky. With floured hands, divide dough and form into 13 even-sized balls. Arrange around edge and in center of cake pan to fill pan.

4 In a small pan over low heat, melt butter. Brush balls of dough with melted butter and sprinkle with brown sugar.

5 Bake for 40 to 50 minutes or until risen and golden brown. Carefully remove from cake pan and let cool on a wire rack.

Chewy Crackles

4

FOR BAKERS
IN THE
FAST LANE

Τhis entire book is devoted to baking that's quick and easy, but in this section we're talking fast with a capital "F". Every one of these recipes will save you time in one way or another. Some need little or no cooking, being "baked" in the refrigerator — an ideal choice for midsummer. (Who wants the kitchen any hotter than it is already in August?) Other recipes save on cleanup time as they mix up quickly in a single bowl. My particular favorite (I hate washing up with a passion) are Gooey Chewy Bars — you mix and bake them in the same pan.

You'll also find a recipe for Chocolate Magic Mix, a wonderful time-saver that lets you whip up your own cake mix to store in the cupboard. Whenever you need a home-bake in a hurry, the mix can be "magically" transformed into a fluffy sponge cake or moist brownies.

So, when time is of the essence — the kids are clamoring for a snack, your mother-in-law "just popped in", or you simply need to satisfy your sweet tooth NOW — give one of these speedy treats a try.

CHOCOLATE TRUFFLE CAKE

Preparation Time
15 minutes
Chilling Time
2 to 3 hours
Makes
one 8-1/2- × 4-1/2-inch (6 cup/1.5 L) cake

This incredibly rich and delicious dessert will comfortably serve six to eight people as a little goes a long way. Cut it in thin slices with a sharp knife and serve with fresh fruit on the side, or top with whipped cream and garnish with cherries.

8 oz	semi-sweet chocolate (see Quick Tip, p.141)	250 g
1/3 cup	butter	75 mL
1	pkg (14.1 oz/400 g) digestive biscuits	1
1/3 cup	granulated sugar	75 mL
1	can (14 oz/398 mL) pears, drained and chopped	1
1	can (5.6 oz/160 mL) evaporated milk (see Quick Tip, p. 63)	1
2	large eggs, beaten	2
	Whipped cream and glacé cherries for decoration	

1 Line a 8-1/2- × 4-1/2-inch (6 cup/1.5 L) loaf pan with foil. This makes it easier to remove the finished cake.

2 In a small bowl over a saucepan of simmering water or in top of double boiler, melt chocolate with butter, stirring occasionally, until smooth. Meanwhile, put digestive biscuits in a large freezer bag and pound with a rolling pin until crushed. (Crushing biscuits this way gives a more interesting texture than if you crush them in a blender or food processor.)

3 Transfer crushed biscuits to a large bowl and stir in sugar and chopped pears. When chocolate has melted, add to biscuit mixture along with evaporated milk and eggs. Mix until ingredients are well combined.

4 Spoon mixture into loaf pan and smooth surface. Chill in refrigerator until set. To serve, carefully loosen cake from loaf pan using foil lining and invert pan onto a flat serving plate. Ease cake from pan, then carefully peel off foil. Decorate with whipped cream and glacé cherries.

It's the easiest thing in the world to burn chocolate when you're melting it, and burnt chocolate is good only for the garbage. The safest method is to break the chocolate into pieces and place in a bowl over a pan of gently simmering water, or in the top half of a double boiler. Make sure the bottom of the bowl (or pan, in the case of a double boiler) doesn't touch the simmering water. When the chocolate has softened, stir until smooth. Take care that no water accidentally falls into the chocolate as this, too, spells disaster.

FRUIT 'N' NUT BARS

Preparation Time
10 minutes
Cooking Time
20 minutes
Makes
8 bars

Use your favorite dried fruit for this recipe: apricots, dates and sultanas are delicious. After being left to cool in the cake pan, the finished bars have a lovely moist consistency.

3 tbsp	butter or margarine	45 mL
1 cup	chopped dried fruit (see Quick Tip, p. 46)	250 mL
2/3 cup	granulated sugar	150 mL
1/2 cup	chopped walnuts	125 mL
1/2 cup	all-purpose flour	125 mL
1 tsp	baking soda dissolved in 2 tbsp (25 mL) milk	5 mL
1	large egg, beaten	1

1 Preheat oven to 350°F (180°C). Have ready a nonstick or lightly greased 8-inch (20 cm) square cake pan.

2 In a medium saucepan over low heat, melt butter. Remove saucepan from heat and add remaining ingredients. Stir until well combined.

3 Spoon mixture into cake pan and smooth surface. Bake for 20 minutes or until golden brown. Let cool in cake pan, then cut into bars when cold.

COFFEE CRUNCH CAKE

Preparation Time
15 minutes
Cooking Time
40 to 45 minutes
Makes
one 8-inch (20 cm) cake

This moist snacking cake has a delicious crunchy topping of pecans and sugar.

1-1/2 cups	all-purpose flour	375 mL
1 cup	firmly packed brown sugar	250 mL
1 cup	butter or margarine (at room temperature)	250 mL
3	large eggs	3
1-1/2 tsp	baking powder	7 mL
3 tbsp	strong black coffee	45 mL
Topping:		
1/2 cup	chopped pecans	125 mL
1/4 cup	granulated sugar	50 mL
2 tbsp	butter	25 mL

1 Preheat oven to 350°F (180°C). Have ready a nonstick or lightly greased 8-inch (20 cm) square cake pan.

2 In a medium bowl, combine all ingredients except those for Topping. Beat together with an electric mixer until well combined. Spoon batter into cake pan and smooth surface.

3 *Topping:* In a blender or food processor fitted with a metal blade, combine all ingredients for Topping and process until mixture is crumbly. (Alternatively, chop pecans finely by hand and, using a fork, mix with sugar and butter until crumbly.)

4 Sprinkle Topping over cake batter. Bake for 40 to 45 minutes until cake shrinks from sides of pan, top springs back when gently pressed, and skewer inserted in the center comes out clean. Let cool completely in pan on a wire rack. Cut into squares to serve.

GOOEY CHEWY BARS

Preparation Time
10 minutes
Cooking Time
30 minutes
Makes
about 14 bars

If ever there was a descriptive name for a recipe, this is it! You'll need to throw caution (and dental care) to the winds when you cook these, but they're worth it and make a popular treat for the kids once in a while. Even better, apart from the baking pan and measuring cup, there's *no* washing up!

1/3 cup	butter or margarine	75 mL
1-1/2 cups	granola	375 mL
1 cup	unsweetened shredded coconut	250 mL
1 cup	mixed dried fruit (sultanas, currants, chopped apricots, etc.)	250 mL
1 cup	chopped glacé cherries	250 mL
1 cup	chopped nuts (walnuts, almonds, etc.)	250 mL
1	can (300 mL) condensed milk (see Quick Tip, p. 63)	1

1 Preheat oven to 350°F (180°C). Place butter in an 11- × 7-inch (28 × 18 cm) jelly roll pan. Place pan in oven for 5 minutes or until butter has melted.

2 Remove pan from oven and sprinkle dry ingredients evenly over melted butter. Drizzle condensed milk evenly over dry ingredients. Return pan to oven and bake for 30 minutes or until golden and bubbling. Let cool in pan and cut into bars when cold.

QUICK TIP

Read the label on the can carefully when buying *condensed* milk or *evaporated* milk. They are different products and won't give the same results in a recipe. Condensed milk is thick, sweet and gooey while evaporated milk is much runnier.

ONE POT TUTTI FRUTTIS

Preparation Time
10 minutes
Cooking Time
8 to 10 minutes
Makes
12 to 15 Tutti Fruttis

Another recipe requiring little washing up, this mixes up quickly in one saucepan. Before baking, the mixture is very runny, so leave at least 3 inches (7.5 cm) of space between each Tutti Frutti on the cookie sheets. Wafer-thin and delicate, these make a sophisticated accompaniment to coffee and go well with vanilla ice cream too.

1/2 cup	butter or margarine	125 mL
3 tbsp	corn syrup	45 mL
3 tbsp	strawberry jam	45 mL
3/4 cup	chopped mixed nuts (walnuts, almonds, etc.)	175 mL
1/4 cup	chopped candied citrus peel	50 mL
1/4 cup	all-purpose flour	50 mL

1 Preheat oven to 350°F (180°C). Have ready two nonstick or lightly greased cookie sheets.

2 In a medium saucepan over medium heat, melt together butter, corn syrup and jam. Remove from heat and stir in all of the remaining ingredients until well combined.

3 Drop teaspoonfuls of the mixture, about 3 inches (7.5 cm) apart, onto cookie sheets. Bake for 8 to 10 minutes until bubbling. Leave on cookie sheets for 2 minutes to firm up, then carefully transfer to wire rack and let cool completely.

NO BAKE FRUITY BARS

Preparation Time
10 minutes
Chilling Time
2 to 3 hours
Makes
8 bars

A good choice during the heat of summer, these chocolaty bars "cook" in the refrigerator so you can avoid turning your kitchen into a Turkish bath. If you can't find rich tea biscuits in your local store, substitute any plain, sweet cookies, such as Basic Icebox Cookies (see p. 40).

8 oz	semi-sweet chocolate (see Quick Tip, p. 141)	250 g
1/4 cup	butter or margarine	50 mL
3 tbsp	corn syrup	45 mL
8 oz	rich tea biscuits (about 22 biscuits)	250 g
1/2 cup	sultana raisins	125 mL
1	orange, grated rind	1

1 Have ready a nonstick or lightly greased 8-inch (20 cm) square cake pan.

2 In a medium bowl over a saucepan of simmering water or in top of double boiler, melt together chocolate, butter and syrup, stirring occasionally, until smooth. Meanwhile, in a blender or food processor fitted with a metal blade, process rich tea biscuits until in fine crumbs.

3 Stir crumbs, sultanas and orange rind into melted chocolate mixture until ingredients are well combined. Spoon into cake pan and smooth surface with back of a spoon. Chill in refrigerator until set, then cut into bars.

CHOCOLATE MAGIC CAKE

Preparation Time
5 minutes
Cooking Time
40 to 45 minutes
Makes
*one 8-inch (20 cm)
round cake*

This light-as-air sponge cake can be decorated with a rich frosting (just double the quantity of the brownie frosting on page 67), or you could fill it with whipped cream and fresh fruit for a scrumptious dessert.

2-1/4 cups	Chocolate Magic Mix (see p. 68)	550 mL
2/3 cup	vegetable oil	150 mL
1/2 cup	milk	125 mL
2 tbsp	corn syrup	25 mL
2	large eggs	2

1 Preheat oven to 300°F (150°C). Have ready a nonstick or lightly greased 8-inch (20 cm) round cake pan.

2 Place Chocolate Magic Mix in large bowl. In a separate medium bowl, beat together all remaining ingredients until smooth and creamy. Add to Chocolate Magic Mix and beat until smooth.

3 Spoon into cake pan and smooth surface. Bake for 40 to 45 minutes or until cake shrinks from sides of pan, top springs back when pressed gently, and skewer inserted in center comes out clean. Turn out and let cool on a wire rack.

QUICK TIP

For perfect cakes every time, have all the ingredients at room temperature before baking, measure them carefully and always use the size and shape of cake pan recommended in the recipe.

CHOCOLATE MAGIC BROWNIES

Preparation Time
10 minutes
Cooking Time
25 minutes
Makes
16 brownies

The fastest frosted brownies in the west! Everyone's favorite takes just minutes to prepare using your Chocolate Magic Mix.

2 cups	Chocolate Magic Mix (see p. 68)	500 mL
2/3 cup	butter or margarine (at room temperature)	150 mL
2	large eggs	2
1/2 tsp	vanilla extract	2 mL
1/2 cup	chopped walnuts	125 mL
Frosting:		
2 oz	semi-sweet chocolate (see Quick Tip, p. 141)	60 g
2 tbsp	milk	25 mL
1/4 cup	butter or margarine (at room temperature)	50 mL
2 cups	icing sugar	500 mL

1 Preheat oven to 350°F (180°C). Have ready a nonstick or lightly greased 8-inch (20 cm) square cake pan.

2 In a medium bowl, beat together Chocolate Magic Mix, butter, eggs and vanilla until smooth and creamy. Stir in walnuts.

3 Spoon into cake pan and smooth surface. Bake for 25 to 30 minutes or until brownies shrink from sides of pan and skewer inserted in the center comes out clean. Let cool in cake pan.

4 *Frosting:* In a small bowl over a pan of simmering water or in top of double boiler, melt chocolate with milk, stirring occasionally, until smooth. In a medium bowl, beat together butter, sugar and melted chocolate until smooth and creamy. Spread Frosting over cooled brownies, then cut into squares.

COCONUT CONES

Preparation Time
10 minutes
Cooking Time
15 to 20 minutes
Makes
about 12 cones

If you like coconut, you'll love these chewy confections, and talk about quick . . . !

1	can (300 mL) condensed milk (see Quick Tip, p. 63)	1
2-1/2- 3 cups	unsweetened shredded coconut	625 to 750 mL
	Few drops red food coloring	
	Glacé cherry halves	

1 Preheat oven to 325°F (160°C). Have ready a nonstick or lightly greased cookie sheet.

2 In a medium bowl, mix together condensed milk and enough coconut.

3 With wet hands, form mixture into small cone shapes, about 2 inches (5 cm) long, and place, standing up on their bases, a little apart, on cookie sheet. Once you've made about six, blend in enough food coloring to remaining mixture to tint it pale pink. Continue making cones until all pink mixture is used. Top each with a cherry half.

4 Bake for 15 to 20 minutes or until cones are tinged with gold. Carefully remove cones from cookie sheet and let cool on a wire rack.

CHEWY CRACKLES

Preparation Time
10 minutes
Chilling Time
2 to 3 hours
Makes
about 10 Crackles

Here's a recipe so quick and easy, I'm almost embarrassed to include it. Variations of these Crackles have been standard fare at children's parties in my family for years and are as popular as ever.

2	jumbo (69.5 g) Oh Henry candy bars, cut in pieces	2
2 tbsp	whipping cream	25 mL
2 cups	cornflakes	500 mL

1 Place about 10 large paper baking cups on a cookie sheet.

2 In a medium saucepan over low heat, melt pieces of Oh Henry bar, stir in cream. Stir in cornflakes until ingredients are well combined. Using two teaspoons, heap mixture in paper baking cups. Chill in the refrigerator until set.

CHOCOLATE MAGIC MIX

Preparation Time
5 minutes
Cooking Time
Nil
Makes
6-1/4 cups (1.55 L)
Magic Mix

If you're a fan of cake mixes and are reluctant to be converted to "baking from scratch", how ever quick and easy, why not whip up your own mix. In fact, it's a shortcut everyone will love. The mix keeps for weeks in an airtight container and can be used to make cakes, cupcakes and brownies. Vary the flavor by replacing the cocoa with flour and adding a little vanilla or almond extract.

4 cups	all-purpose flour	1 L
2 tsp	baking powder	10 mL
2 tsp	baking soda	10 mL
6-1/2 tbsp plus 2 tsp	unsweetened cocoa powder	100 mL
2 cups	firmly packed brown sugar	500 mL

1 In a large bowl, sift together flour, baking powder, baking soda and cocoa. Stir in sugar. Spoon into an airtight container and store in a cool, dry place.

Quick Brown Rolls

5

WHOLLY DELICIOUS

Baking that's good for you? Come on, who am I trying to kid! When you consider the oodles of fat and sugar in some recipes, it's hard to believe some baked goods can be nutritious as well as delicious.

Whole wheat flour isn't just for health food fanatics anymore. Its wonderfully nutty taste can add a unique flavor to all kinds of home-bakes. What's more, whole wheat cakes and breads are an appetizing way to include that singularly *un*appetizing (but essential) health-giving item — fibre — in your diet.

If you think whole wheat baking means indigestible confrontations with dirty brown pastry that tastes as bad as it looks, or loaves of bread disguised as house bricks, it's time to look again! Here are delicious muffins, crisp cookies, rich shortbread and even light-as-air cakes that are as far removed from stodgy food (and bricks!) as possible.

Although a diet consisting entirely of whole wheat home-bakes is not recommended, if you have to indulge in lots of lovely calories (and don't we all once in a while?), it's nice to know those wholesome cakes and breads are doing you some good!

APPLE NUT MUFFINS

Preparation Time
15 minutes

Cooking Time
15 to 20 minutes

Makes
about 10 muffins

What a relief to find something the kids love that's actually good for them! Crunchy peanut butter adds a nutty texture to these wholesome and delicious muffins, and is high in protein — 2 tablespoons (25 mL) contain as much protein as an egg.

1/2 cup	wheat germ	125 mL
1/2 cup	hot water	125 mL
3/4 cup	all-purpose flour	175 mL
1/2 cup	whole wheat flour	125 mL
1-1/2 tsp	baking soda	7 mL
1/4 tsp	salt	1 mL
1/4 tsp	ground cinnamon	1 mL
3/4 cup	firmly packed brown sugar	175 mL
1/4 cup	crunchy peanut butter	50 mL
1/4 cup	shortening (at room temperature)	50 mL
1	large egg	1
1/2 cup	milk	125 mL
1/2 cup	applesauce	125 mL
	Chopped peanuts for decoration	

1 Preheat oven to 375°F (190°C). Have ready a nonstick, lightly greased or paper-lined 12-cup muffin pan.

2 Place wheat germ in small bowl. Pour hot water over and set aside.

3 In a medium bowl, mix together flours, baking soda, salt and cinnamon.

4 In a separate bowl, beat together sugar, peanut butter, shortening, egg, milk and applesauce until smooth. Add dry ingredients and wheat germ and mix until just moistened.

5 Spoon into muffin cups, filling each about three-quarters full. Top each muffin with a few chopped peanuts. Bake for 15 to 20 minutes or until risen and browned. Turn out of muffin pan and let cool on a wire rack.

QUICK TIP

For light, moist muffins, stir the batter until the dry ingredients are only *just* moistened. Over-mixing results in tough muffins with large holes in them.

ROLLED-OAT CAKES

Preparation Time
15 minutes
Cooking Time
30 minutes
Makes
about 10 oat cakes

In Scotland, the ubiquitous oatcake is served as a snack with a hunk of cheese or crumbled into homemade soup. Genuine oatcakes are a bit tricky to make but my husband, a Scot, claims that this simpler version is the next best thing.

1/3 cup	shortening	75 mL
2 cups	rolled oats	500 mL
3/4 cup	whole wheat flour	175 mL
1 tsp	baking powder	5 mL
1/2 tsp	salt	2 mL
1/3 cup	water (approx)	75 mL

1 Preheat oven to 350°F (180°C). Have ready two nonstick or lightly greased cookie sheets.

2 In a small saucepan over medium heat, melt shortening. Set aside to cool. In a medium bowl, mix together oats, flour, baking powder, and salt. Mix in cooled shortening and enough water to form a stiff dough.

3 Turn out dough onto a lightly floured surface and knead lightly for 2 to 3 minutes until dough holds together. Roll out into 1/4-inch (5 mm) thickness. With a 3-inch (7 cm) floured cookie cutter, cut out rounds and arrange, about 1 inch (2.5 cm) apart, on baking sheets. Bake for 30 minutes or until tinged with gold. Transfer to wire rack and let cool.

BANANA HONEY CAKE

Preparation Time
20 minutes
Cooking Time
40 to 45 minutes
Makes
one 8-inch (20 cm)
round cake

If you have a couple of over-the-hill bananas that have been hanging around in the fruit bowl for too long, this is a good way to use them up. The combination of all-purpose and whole wheat flours in this recipe provides nutritious fibre in a light and airy sponge cake. A delicious (but definitely *not* nutritious) alternative filling would be chocolate frosting or whipped cream.

3/4 cup	all-purpose flour	175 mL
1/2 cup	whole wheat flour	125 mL
1 tsp	baking soda	5 mL
1/2 tsp	baking powder	2 mL
1/4 tsp	grated nutmeg	1 mL
Pinch	salt	Pinch
1/2 cup	liquid honey	125 mL
2 tbsp	butter or margarine (at room temperature)	25 mL
1/4 cup	firmly packed brown sugar	50 mL
2	large eggs	2
1	large ripe banana, peeled and mashed	1
Filling:		
1	large ripe banana	1
Dash	lemon juice	Dash
1/2 cup	sour cream	125 mL
1 tbsp	liquid honey	15 mL
	Icing sugar	

1 Preheat oven to 325°F (160°C). Have ready a nonstick or lightly greased 8-inch (20 cm) round cake pan.

2 In a medium bowl, mix together flours, baking soda, baking powder, nutmeg and salt. In a separate bowl, beat together honey, butter and sugar until smooth and creamy. Beat in eggs, one at a time. Gradually stir dry ingredients alternately with the mashed banana into honey mixture.

3 Pour batter into cake pan and smooth surface. Bake for 40 to 45 minutes or until cake shrinks from sides of pan, top springs back when pressed gently, and skewer inserted in center comes out clean. Turn out and let cool on a wire rack.

4 *Filling:* In a small bowl, mash banana with lemon juice until smooth. Stir in sour cream and honey. Cut cake in half horizontally, spread filling in middle and replace top. Dredge top of cake with icing sugar.

WHOLE WHEAT CRACKERS

Preparation Time
10 minutes
Cooking Time
10 minutes
Makes
about 15 crackers

Quick-to-make, these little bite-sized snacking crackers have the delicious nutty taste of whole wheat flour which makes them the perfect partner for sharp Cheddar cheese.

1 cup	whole wheat flour	250 mL
1 tsp	baking powder	5 mL
1/2 tsp	salt	2 mL
1/3 cup	butter or margarine	75 mL
3 tbsp	firmly packed brown sugar	45 mL
3 tbsp	milk (approx)	45 mL

1 Preheat oven to 375°F (190°C). Have ready a nonstick or lightly greased cookie sheet.

2 In a medium bowl, mix together flour, baking powder and salt. With your fingertips or pastry blender, rub in butter until mixture resembles fine crumbs. Stir in sugar and enough milk to form a stiff dough.

3 Turn out dough onto a lightly floured surface and knead for about 2 minutes or until free of cracks. Roll out to 1/4-inch (5 mm) thickness and prick all over with a wooden toothpick. With a 2-1/2-inch (6 cm) floured cookie cutter, cut into rounds and arrange, about 2 inches (5 cm) apart, on cookie sheet. Bake for 10 minutes or until golden. Transfer to wire rack and let cool.

QUICK BROWN ROLLS

Preparation Time
25 minutes
(excluding rising)
Cooking Time
20 minutes
Makes
about 15 rolls

Most recipes that require yeast are fairly time-consuming to prepare but this short-cut turns out good, old-fashioned home-baked bread rolls in a fraction of the time.

2-1/4 cups	warm water	550 mL
1-1/2 tsp	quick-rising yeast	7 mL
1-1/2 tsp	liquid honey	7 mL
5 cups	whole wheat flour	1.25 L
1 tsp	salt	5 mL
	Toppings (see Quick Tip, p. 56)	

1 Measure 2 tbsp (25 mL) of the water into a cup. Sprinkle yeast over water. Leave in a warm place for 2 minutes. Stir in honey and leave for 15 minutes longer until frothy.

2 In a large bowl, mix together flour and salt. Add frothy yeast mixture and remaining water. Mix well with your hands until dough feels smooth and elastic and leaves sides of bowl clean.

3 Turn out onto a lightly floured surface and knead lightly for 3 to 5 minutes or until dough is free of cracks. Divide into about 15 equal pieces and shape into balls or as desired (see Quick Tip, p. 76). Place on cookie sheet far enough apart for balls to double in size. Cover with a clean tea towel and leave in a warm place for 20 minutes or until doubled in size. Preheat oven to 400°F (200°C).

4 Add toppings to rolls, if desired (see Quick Tip, p. 76). Bake for about 20 minutes until golden, and rolls sound hollow when tapped on bottoms. Let cool on a wire rack.

QUICK TIP

You can have great fun shaping dough from homemade rolls — form them into the initials of family members or just let your imagination run riot. Here are a few other suggestions:
Knots — roll piece of dough between the palms of your hands to make a sausage shape, then tie in a knot.
Cottage Rolls — divide each piece of dough into a large and small piece and shape into balls. Place the small ball on top of the large and, with a

floured finger, poke a hole through the top, right down to the work surface, to join the two balls together.

Bloomers—shape each piece of dough into an oval. With a sharp knife, cut two or three slashes in the top of each.

Braids—divide each piece of dough into three equal portions and roll each between the palms of your hands to make a sausage shape. Join the three at one end and braid together, tucking ends under.

Different toppings can turn even simple round rolls into something special. For a soft-topped roll, simply dredge with flour. Crispier rolls can be created by brushing them with beaten egg, then sprinkling them with one of the following: sesame, poppy or caraway seeds; grated cheese; coarsely ground black pepper; sea salt; brown sugar.

GOOD-FOR-YOU BARS

Preparation Time
10 minutes

Cooking Time
20 to 25 minutes

Makes
8 bars

These chewy bars are aptly named. Team one with a glass of ice-cold milk for a great "meal in a hurry".

1/2 cup	butter or margarine	125 mL
1/2 cup	firmly packed brown sugar	125 mL
1/3 cup	corn syrup	75 mL
3/4 cup	rolled oats	175 mL
1/2 cup	sultanas	125 mL
1/2 cup	unsweetened shredded coconut	125 mL
1/2 cup	chopped mixed nuts (walnuts, almonds, pecans, etc.)	125 mL

1 Preheat oven to 350°F (180°C). Have ready a nonstick or lightly greased 8-inch (20 cm) square cake pan.

2 In a medium saucepan over low heat, melt butter with sugar and syrup. Stir in remaining ingredients until well combined.

3 Spoon into cake pan and smooth with back of a spoon. Bake for 20 to 25 minutes or until golden brown and bubbling. Leave in pan for 2 minutes to firm up, then score into bars with a knife. Let cool completely in cake pan. Break into bars when cold.

APRICOT CRUMBLE SQUARES

Preparation Time
25 minutes
Cooking Time
25 minutes
Makes
9 squares

Served slightly warm, these spicy, fruit-filled squares make a delicious dessert topped with cream or ice cream. Or let them cool and eat as a nutritious snack.

1-1/2 cups	finely chopped dried apricots (see Quick Tip, p. 46)	375 mL
2 tbsp	water	25 mL
2 tbsp	liquid honey	25 mL
1 tbsp	lemon juice	15 mL
1/4 tsp	grated nutmeg	1 mL
1-1/2 cups	whole wheat flour	375 mL
3/4 cup	butter or margarine	175 mL
1/3 cup	firmly packed brown sugar	75 mL

1 Preheat oven to 350°F (180°C). Have ready a nonstick or lightly greased 8-inch (20 cm) square cake pan.

2 In a small saucepan over high heat, bring apricots, water, honey, lemon juice and nutmeg to boil. Reduce heat, cover pan and simmer for 15 minutes or until apricots are soft and pulpy.

3 Meanwhile, place flour in a medium bowl. With your fingertips or pastry blender, rub in butter until mixture resembles fine crumbs. Stir in sugar.

4 Press half of the mixture onto base of cake pan, smoothing surface. Cover evenly with cooked apricots. Sprinkle remaining flour mixture over apricots and press down lightly with palms of your hands.

5 Bake for 25 minutes or until golden brown. Cut into squares while still warm. Leave in cake pan for 5 minutes to firm up, then carefully transfer to a wire rack and let cool completely.

WHOLE WHEAT HONEY SHORTBREAD

Preparation Time
10 minutes
Cooking Time
30 minutes
Makes
8 wedges

For the rich, authentic taste of real Scottish shortbread, you must use butter for this recipe. It may seem extravagant — until you taste the result!

1-1/2 cups	whole wheat flour	375 mL
3/4 cup	butter	175 mL
1/3 cup	firmly packed brown sugar	75 mL
1 tbsp	liquid honey	15 mL

1 Preheat oven to 325°F (160°C). Have ready a nonstick or lightly greased cookie sheet. Place flour in a medium bowl and with your fingertips or pastry blender, rub in butter until mixture resembles fine crumbs. Stir in sugar, then add honey. With a fork, mix until dough holds together.

2 Turn out dough onto a lightly floured surface and knead for a few seconds until free of cracks. Dough will tend to be crumbly but the warmth of your hands will help it bind together. Place dough on cookie sheet and pat out into a round about 1/2-inch (1 cm) thick. Pinch edge between your thumb and forefinger to make a decorative border all around and prick dough all over with a fork. With a sharp knife, score into 8 wedges.

3 Bake for 30 minutes or until light brown at edges. Leave on cookie sheet for 5 minutes to firm up, then cut into wedges. Transfer wedges to wire rack and let cool completely.

SESAME SNAPS

Preparation Time
10 minutes
Cooking Time
15 to 20 minutes
Makes
12 to 15 cookies

These crispiest, crunchiest of cookies are packed with the goodness of sesame seeds and whole wheat flour. Their caramel flavor will make them a surefire winner with the children.

1 tbsp	liquid honey	15 mL
1/2 cup	butter or margarine	125 mL
1/2 cup	firmly packed brown sugar	125 mL
1 cup	whole wheat flour	250 mL
1/3 cup	sesame seeds	75 mL
2 tsp	baking soda dissolved in 1 tbsp (15 mL) milk	10 mL

1 Preheat oven to 300°F (150°C). Have ready two nonstick or lightly greased cookie sheets.

2 In a small saucepan over medium heat, heat honey, butter and sugar until butter has melted. Allow to boil briefly, then remove from heat.

3 Add flour, sesame seeds and dissolved baking soda to pan and stir until well combined.

4 Drop teaspoonfuls of mixture, about 3 inches (8 cm) apart, onto cookie sheets. Bake for 15 to 20 minutes or until golden brown. Leave on cookie sheet for 2 minutes to firm up, then transfer to wire rack and let cool completely.

QUICK TIP

Store crisp cookies, such as Sesame Snaps, in a container with a loose-fitting lid. If the cookies become soft, simply crisp them up by baking for 5 minutes in a 300°F (150°C) oven.

MALTED SLAB CAKE

Preparation Time
15 minutes
Cooking Time
30 minutes
Makes
one 8-inch (20 cm) square cake

Many recipes using whole wheat flour tend to be hearty (some even verge on "solid"). However, this light, airy spongecake is anything but. Malted milk drink powder gives an interesting flavor and the quick-mix frosting adds the finishing touch.

1-1/4 cups	whole wheat flour	300 mL
1/3 cup	Ovaltine	75 mL
1 tbsp	baking powder	15 mL
3/4 cup	butter or margarine (at room temperature)	175 mL
1/3 cup	firmly packed brown sugar	75 mL
2	large eggs	2
1/2 cup	milk	125 mL
Glaze:		
3/4 cup	sifted icing sugar	175 mL
1/4 cup	Ovaltine	50 mL
2 tbsp	milk	25 mL
	Slivered almonds for decoration	

1 Preheat oven to 350°F (180°C). Have ready a nonstick or lightly greased 8-inch (20 cm) square cake pan.

2 In a small bowl, mix together flour, Ovaltine and baking powder. In a separate bowl, beat together butter and sugar until pale beige and fluffy. Beat in eggs, one at a time. Fold in dry ingredients alternately with milk until mixture is well-blended and of soft, dropping consistency.

3 Pour batter into cake pan and smooth surface. Bake for 30 minutes or until cake shrinks away from sides of pan, and a skewer inserted in center comes out clean. Leave in cake pan for 2 minutes, then turn out and let cool completely on a wire rack.

4 *Glaze:* In a medium bowl, beat together sugar, Ovaltine and milk until smooth. Pour over cooled cake, spreading to edges with a knife dipped in hot water. Decorate with slivered almonds.

Glazed Walnut Apricot Cake

6

GOOEY AND GORGEOUS

If you're looking for an economical snacking cake or an unspectacular finish to a "ho-hum" meal, perhaps you should skip the next few pages. Here's the part of the book where we throw caution to the wind and indulge. The recipes in this section are suffering from minor identity crises — are they dreamy desserts or simply lavish coffee-time treats? In fact, they're both.

Delightfully rich and spectacular, these cakes, gâteaux and tartlets are as easy to prepare as the other home-bakes in this book. Some may take a few extra minutes to decorate but the results are well worth it.

The goodies that follow are at their best when freshly baked, although you can store them, undecorated, for a couple of days in an airtight container, or freeze them (see p. 22). Frost and decorate them shortly before serving.

I make no apologies for these recipes — they're sinfully rich and criminally calorific. What's more, they're irresistible. Even my husband's rigidly unsweet tooth couldn't muster enough defenses against these temptations — he even asked for "seconds"!

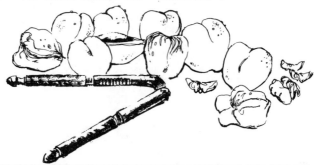

BRANDY ALEXANDER GÂTEAU

Preparation Time
25 minutes
Cooking Time
30 to 35 minutes
Makes
one 8-inch (20 cm) round cake, 6 to 8 servings

One of my favorite cocktails, that delightful concoction of cream, brandy and nutmeg, was the inspiration behind this cake. A hint of spice and brandy flavoring teams perfectly with the rich, chocolaty frosting. For a special occasion, you could add a layer of whipped cream to the filling or serve the cake with table cream.

3/4 cup	granulated sugar	175 mL
1/3 cup	butter or margarine (at room temperature)	75 mL
2	large eggs	2
1/2 tsp	brandy extract	2 mL
1-1/2 cups	all-purpose flour	375 mL
2 tsp	baking powder	10 mL
1/4 tsp	salt	1 mL
1/2 tsp	grated nutmeg	2 mL
1/2 cup	milk	125 mL

Chocolate Frosting:

12 oz	semi-sweet chocolate (see Quick Tip, p. 141)	350 g
2 tbsp	butter or margarine	25 mL
3-1/3 cups	icing sugar, sifted	825 mL
1/2 cup	milk	125 mL
1/2 tsp	brandy extract	2 mL

Decoration:

8 to 10	walnut halves	8 to 10
	Icing sugar	

1 Preheat oven to 350°F (180°C). Have ready two nonstick or lightly greased 8-inch (20 cm) round cake pans.

2 In a medium bowl, beat together sugar and butter until pale yellow and fluffy. Add eggs, one at a time, beating well after each addition. Beat in brandy extract.

3 In a separate medium bowl, sift together flour, baking powder, salt and nutmeg. With a metal spoon, carefully fold one-third of the flour mixture, followed by one-third of the milk into creamed mixture. Repeat until all flour mixture and milk are used and a smooth batter is formed.

4 Divide batter between cake pans and smooth surface. Bake for 25 to 30 minutes or until cakes shrink away from side of pans and skewer inserted in centers comes out clean. Let cool in pans for 5 minutes, then turn out and let cool completely on a wire rack.

5 *Chocolate Frosting:* In a large bowl over a saucepan of simmering water or in top of double boiler, melt chocolate with butter, stirring occasionally, until smooth. Remove bowl or top of double boiler from heat and gradually beat in icing sugar, milk and brandy extract until smooth.

6 Cut cakes in half horizontally. Spread base of one with one-quarter of the frosting. Slice a little from top half of cake to level surface, if necessary, and invert on top of frosted layer. Spread with another quarter of frosting and top with bottom layer of second cake. Spread with another quarter of frosting. Top with remaining layer of cake and spread with rest of frosting. Dredge walnut halves with icing sugar and arrange around top of cake to decorate.

QUICK TIP

When creaming butter and sugar together for a cake, you'll achieve a lighter, fluffier texture if you rinse the mixing bowl and beaters in hot water, then dry thoroughly, before you begin.

STRAWBERRY PUFF

Preparation Time
25 minutes
Cooking Time
40 minutes
Makes
one 8-inch (20 cm) round Strawberry Puff, 6 servings

Whoever invented choux pastry should be awarded a medal. Never has anything so easy to make produced such spectacular results. The gooey uncooked pastry rises to crispy lightness in the oven. Don't fill the choux pastry ring until just before serving in case it becomes soggy. Strawberry Puff serves more people and looks especially attractive if you fill the center with fresh strawberries dusted with icing sugar.

Choux Pastry:

2/3 cup	water	150 mL
1/4 cup PLUS 2 tsp	butter or margarine	60 mL
1/2 cup	all-purpose flour	125 mL
2	large eggs	2

Strawberry Filling:

1 cup	hulled strawberries (fresh or frozen and thawed)	250 mL
	Milk	
2	large eggs, separated (see Quick Tip, p. 129)	2
1/3 cup	granulated sugar	75 mL
2 tbsp	all-purpose flour	25 mL
2 tbsp	cornstarch	25 mL
1	small orange, grated rind	1
	Icing sugar for decoration	

1 Preheat oven to 400°F (200°C). Have ready a nonstick or lightly greased 8-inch (20 cm) round cake pan.

2 *Choux Pastry:* In a medium saucepan over medium heat, stir together water and butter until butter has melted. Increase heat and bring to boil. Remove from heat and immediately add flour, all at once. With a wooden spoon, beat well until mixture forms a ball and leaves side of pan clean. Add eggs, one at a time, beating well until a smooth, glossy paste is formed.

3 Spoon mixture evenly around edge of cake pan to form a ring, leaving a space in the center. Bake for 40 minutes or until well risen and golden brown. Carefully remove choux pastry ring from pan. Make a small horizontal slit in the side to allow steam to escape, and let cool on a wire rack.

4 *Strawberry Filling:* In a blender or food processor fitted with a metal blade, purée strawberries until smooth. (Alternatively, press fruit through a sieve.) Transfer strawberry purée to a 2-cup (500 mL) measure and stir in enough milk to make 1-1/3 cups (325 mL).

5 Return 1/3 cup (75 mL) strawberry/milk mixture to blender or food processor. Add egg yolks, sugar, flour and cornstarch and process until smooth. (Alternatively, in a medium bowl, beat ingredients until smooth.)

6 Meanwhile, in a medium saucepan over medium heat, heat remaining 1 cup (250 mL) strawberry/milk mixture until just below boiling point. Remove pan from heat and stir in egg yolk mixture. Return to heat and slowly bring to boil, stirring continuously, until mixture is smooth and thick. Remove pan from heat. Stir in orange rind and let mixture cool slightly.

7 In a medium bowl, whisk egg whites with a wire whisk or electric mixer until they stand in stiff peaks. With a metal spoon, carefully fold egg whites into strawberry mixture until well combined. Let cool completely.

8 With a sharp knife, carefully cut choux pastry ring in half horizontally. With a teaspoon, scoop out and discard any soft dough from both halves of pastry ring to make room for filling. Spoon Strawberry Filling evenly into bottom half of ring and replace top. Sift icing sugar over top to decorate.

ORANGE JEWEL CAKE

Preparation Time
30 minutes
Cooking Time
35 to 40 minutes
Makes
one 8-inch (20 cm) round cake, 6 to 8 servings

This quick-mix cake uses concentrated orange juice to add a citrus tang. Chunks of golden caramelized sugar make a sparkling decoration and add interesting crunch. If you're short of time, omit the caramel — the cake will be almost as good.

Cake:

2 cups	all-purpose flour	500 mL
1 cup	granulated sugar	250 mL
1 cup	frozen concentrated orange juice, thawed	250 mL
1/2 cup	butter or margarine (at room temperature)	125 mL
2	large eggs	2
1-1/2 tsp	baking powder	7 mL
1/2 tsp	baking soda	2 mL
1/2 tsp	salt	2 mL

Caramel:

1 cup	granulated sugar	250 mL

Orange Frosting:

4-1/2 cups	icing sugar, sifted	1.125 L
1/3 cup	butter (at room temperature)	75 mL
1/4 cup	frozen concentrated orange juice, thawed	50 mL
1	orange, grated rind	1

1 Preheat oven to 350°F (180°C). Have ready a nonstick or lightly greased 8-inch (20 cm) round cake pan.

2 *Cake:* In a large bowl, beat together all ingredients for cake, until smooth. Spoon into cake pan and smooth surface. Bake for 35 to 40 minutes or until cake shrinks from side of pan and skewer inserted in center comes out clean. Let cool in pan for 5 minutes, then turn out and let cool completely on a wire rack.

3 *Caramel:* Have ready a nonstick or lightly greased 10-1/2 × 6-1/2-inch (26.5 × 16.5 cm) cookie sheet.

4 In a small, heavy saucepan over medium heat, heat sugar, stirring occasionally, until completely melted. Bring to boil and immediately pour onto cookie sheet. Tilt sheet to spread caramel evenly. Set aside to harden.

5 *Orange Frosting:* In a large bowl, beat together all ingredients until smooth and creamy. Cut cake in half horizontally and spread with one-third of frosting.

6 Break caramel into pieces. Put half of the pieces in a folded tea towel and crush finely by pounding with a rolling pin. Sprinkle crushed caramel over frosting on bottom layer. Replace top of cake and spread remaining frosting over top and sides. Decorate top of cake with remaining pieces of caramel.

QUICK TIP

For easy cleanup when frosting round cakes, choose a serving plate about 2 inches (5 cm) larger than the cake. Cut a circle of waxed paper about 1 inch (2.5 cm) larger than the plate. Cut out a circle from the center of the paper so you're left with about a 3 inch (7 cm) wide ring of waxed paper. Put the ring on the plate and top with cake. Frost the cake, then pull away the paper — presto, a clean serving plate!

SUMMER UPSIDE-DOWN CAKE

Preparation Time
15 minutes
Cooking Time
35 minutes
Makes
one 8-inch (20 cm) round cake, 8 servings

A new twist to an old favorite, this upside-down cake turns out to reveal an unusual topping of kiwifruit and raspberries. It's best served slightly warm with cream but is also delicious cold. You could also whip up a speedy raspberry sauce by pressing 1 cup (250 mL) raspberries through a sieve, then sweetening to taste with icing sugar. Add a little flare with a dash of brandy or your favorite liqueur.

Base:

1/4 cup	butter	50 mL
1/3 cup	packed brown sugar	75 mL
2	kiwifruit, sliced	2
1 cup	raspberries (fresh or frozen and thawed)	250 mL

Cake:

1-1/2 cups	all-purpose flour	375 mL
1/2 cup	granulated sugar	125 mL
1/3 cup	unsweetened shredded coconut	75 mL
2 tsp	baking powder	10 mL
1/2 tsp	salt	2 mL
1/4 cup	butter or margarine (at room temperature)	50 mL
1/2 cup	milk	125 mL
2	large eggs	2
1	lemon, grated rind	1

1 Preheat oven to 350°F (180°C).

2 *Base:* In an 8-3/4-inch (22 cm) pie plate, melt butter in oven for 5 minutes. Stir in brown sugar. Arrange slices of kiwifruit around edge of base of plate. Arrange raspberries in center.

3 *Cake:* In a large bowl, beat together all ingredients until smooth. Spoon cake batter evenly over fruit, spreading to cover completely.

4 Bake for about 30 minutes or until cake shrinks from side of plate and top is golden brown. Let cool in plate for 5 minutes, then place a flat serving plate over pie plate and invert to turn cake out onto plate.

QUICK TIP

Don't panic if you run out of baking powder on baking day—make your own. To each cup (250 mL) of all-purpose flour, add 2 tsp (10 mL) cream of tartar, 1 tsp (5 mL) baking soda, and 1/2 tsp (2 mL) salt.

QUICK TIP

Need sour cream for a recipe but only have fresh? Add a little vinegar or lemon juice to fresh cream (one part vinegar or lemon juice to five parts cream) and let stand in a warm place for 30 minutes.

SPICY APPLE ROLL

Preparation Time
30 minutes
Cooking Time
20 to 25 minutes
Makes
one 8-inch-long (20 cm) roll, 6 to 8 servings

This upscale version of that old faithful, the jelly roll, has a delicious creamy apple filling. For an extra-special touch, instead of dredging the finished roll with icing sugar, pipe whipped cream over the roll and sprinkle with a little ground cinnamon.

3/4 cup	all-purpose flour	175 mL
1 tsp	baking powder	5 mL
1/2 tsp	ground cinnamon	2 mL
1/4 tsp	salt	1 mL
3	large eggs	3
2/3 cup	granulated sugar	150 mL
3 tbsp	warm water	45 mL
	Icing sugar	
Filling:		
1 cup	sour cream	250 mL
1/2 cup	applesauce	125 mL
	Icing sugar for decoration	

1 Preheat oven to 375°F (190°C). Line base and sides of a 13- × 9- × 1/2-inch (33 × 23 × 1.25 cm) jelly roll pan with waxed paper.

2 In a medium bowl, sift together flour, baking powder, cinnamon and salt.

3 In a large bowl, beat eggs with an electric mixer for 5 minutes until pale yellow and very fluffy. Gradually beat in sugar, then water until thick and creamy.

4 With a metal spoon, gradually fold flour mixture into egg mixture until ingredients are well combined. Spoon mixture evenly into jelly roll pan. Bake for 20 to 25 minutes or until cake springs back when pressed gently.

5 Spread out a clean tea towel on work surface and sift evenly with icing sugar. Invert jelly roll pan onto tea towel. Remove pan from cake and carefully peel off waxed paper. With a sharp knife, trim off crisp edges. Starting from a short edge, carefully roll up cake and towel together, but not too tightly. Let cool completely on a wire rack.

6 *Filling:* In a small bowl, mix together sour cream and applesauce until well combined. When cake is cold, carefully unroll it and spread with filling. Re-roll cake without tea towel. Place on a serving plate, seam side down, and sift icing sugar over to decorate.

CARIBBEAN BANANA SHORTCAKE

Preparation Time
25 minutes
Cooking Time
20 minutes
Makes
one 8-inch (20 cm) shortcake, 6 to 8 servings

Even hard-core traditionalists have been known to forsake their favorite strawberry shortcake for this "tropical" version. The delicately coffee-flavored shortcake is the perfect partner for the rich banana cream. The liqueur in the filling can be replaced by strong, black coffee, if you prefer.

1-3/4 cups	all-purpose flour	425 mL
1 tbsp	baking powder	15 mL
1/4 tsp	salt	1 mL

1/2 cup	butter	125 mL
1/2 cup	granulated sugar	125 mL
1	large egg	1
2 tbsp	milk	25 mL
2 tsp	instant coffee granules	10 mL

Banana Cream Filling:

2	ripe bananas	2
1 tbsp	granulated sugar	15 mL
1 tsp	lemon juice	5 mL
3/4 cup	whipping cream	175 mL
2 tbsp	coffee liqueur	25 mL

Decoration:

1	ripe banana	1
1 tbsp	lemon juice	15 mL

1 Preheat oven to 375°F (190°C). Have ready a nonstick or lightly greased 8-inch (20 cm) round cake pan.

2 In a medium bowl, sift together flour, baking powder and salt. With your fingertips or pastry blender, rub in butter until mixture resembles fine crumbs. Stir in sugar.

3 In a small bowl, beat together egg, milk and coffee. Add to flour mixture and stir with a fork until mixture clings together and ingredients are well combined. Tip mixture into cake pan and press with palms of your hands until surface is level. Bake for 20 minutes or until light golden and firm. Let cool in pan for 5 minutes, then turn out and let cool completely on a wire rack.

4 *Banana Cream Filling:* Peel bananas and cut into chunks. In a blender or food processor fitted with a metal blade, process bananas, sugar and lemon juice until smooth. (Alternatively, in a medium bowl, mash all ingredients with fork until smooth.)

5 In a medium bowl, whip cream until it stands in soft peaks. With a metal spoon, carefully fold in banana mixture, then liqueur, until ingredients are well combined.

6 Cut shortcake in half horizontally. Spread bottom layer with half of the Banana Cream Filling and replace top. Spread with remaining Banana Cream Filling.

7 *Decoration:* Peel and slice banana and toss with lemon juice. Arrange slices around top of cake to decorate.

GLAZED WALNUT APRICOT CAKE

Preparation Time
25 minutes

Cooking Time
30 to 35 minutes

Makes
one 8-inch (20 cm) round cake, 6 to 8 servings

This is the best kind of gâteau. It's simple to make and decorate, but the finished cake with its shiny topping of glazed apricots and crunchy nutty coating looks very professional. Once decorated, serve the cake as soon as possible as the cream cheese tends to crack.

3/4 cup	granulated sugar	175 mL
1/3 cup	butter or margarine (at room temperature)	75 mL
2	large eggs	2
1 tsp	almond extract	5 mL
1-1/2 cups	all-purpose flour	375 mL
2 tsp	baking powder	10 mL
1/4 tsp	salt	1 mL
1/2 cup	milk	125 mL
Filling:		
1	pkg (250 g) cream cheese (at room temperature)	1
1 tbsp	liquid honey	15 mL
1 tsp	lemon juice	5 mL
Glaze:		
1/2 cup	apricot jam	125 mL
2 tbsp	water	25 mL
1 cup	finely chopped walnuts	250 mL
1	can (14 oz/398 mL) apricot halves, well drained	1

1 Preheat oven to 350°F (180°C). Have ready a nonstick or lightly greased 8-inch (20 cm) round cake pan.

2 In a medium bowl, beat together sugar and butter until pale yellow and fluffy. Add eggs, one at a time, beating well after each addition. Beat in almond extract.

3 In a separate medium bowl, sift together flour, baking powder and salt. With a metal spoon, carefully fold one-third of the flour mixture, followed by one-third of the milk into creamed mixture. Repeat until all flour mixture and milk are used and a smooth batter is formed.

---

4 Spoon batter into cake pan and smooth surface. Bake for 30 to 35 minutes or until cake shrinks away from side of pan and skewer inserted in center comes out clean. Let cool in pan for 5 minutes, then turn out and let cool completely on a wire rack.

---

5 *Filling:* In a blender or food processor fitted with a metal blade, process cream cheese, honey and lemon juice until smooth and creamy. (Alternatively, in a medium bowl, blend all ingredients with a wooden spoon until smooth.)

---

6 Just before serving, cut cake in half horizontally and spread bottom layer with half cream cheese mixture. Replace top.

---

7 *Glaze:* In a small saucepan over high heat, bring apricot jam and water to boil and boil for 3 minutes. Brush sides of cake with some of glaze. Sprinkle walnuts over a flat plate. Turn cake on its side and roll in walnuts until side of cake is evenly coated. Place cake on a serving plate.

---

8 Spread remaining cream cheese mixture over top of cake. Arrange apricot halves, cut sides down, over cream cheese and brush with remaining glaze. Sprinkle any leftover walnuts over glazed apricots.

GOOEY CHOCOLATE CHERRY CAKE

Preparation Time
20 minutes
Cooking Time
30 minutes
Makes
one 8-inch (20 cm) round cake, 6 to 8 servings

Another of my mother's wonderful creations, this recipe is a great morale-booster for the not-so-great cook. When you take it from the oven, the cake should be slightly sunken in the middle and still fairly sticky.

6 oz	semi-sweet chocolate (see Quick Tip, p. 141)	175 g
2 tbsp	milk	25 mL
3/4 cup	granulated sugar	175 mL
1/2 cup	butter (at room temperature)	125 mL
3	large eggs	3
2/3 cup	all-purpose flour	150 mL
1 tsp	baking powder	5 mL
Filling:		
1 cup	whipping cream	250 mL
1	can (14 oz/398 mL) pitted cherries, drained	1

1 Preheat oven to 350°F (180°C). Have ready a nonstick or lightly greased 8-inch (20 cm) round cake pan.

2 In a small bowl over a saucepan of simmering water or in top of double boiler, melt 4 ounces (125 g) of the chocolate with milk, stirring occasionally until smooth.

3 Meanwhile, in a medium bowl, beat together sugar and butter until pale yellow and fluffy. Add eggs, one at a time, beating well after each addition. Stir in melted chocolate. Sift in flour and baking powder and fold in with a metal spoon until ingredients are well combined.

4 Spoon batter into cake pan and smooth surface. Bake for 20 minutes, then cover cake with a sheet of aluminum foil. Bake for 10 minutes longer or until cake shrinks from side of pan and center has sunk slightly.

Let cool completely in cake pan, then remove from pan and cut in half horizontally.

5 *Filling:* In a medium bowl, whip cream until it stands in soft peaks. Spread three-quarters of the cream over bottom layer of cake and cover evenly with three-quarters of the cherries. Replace top of cake. Fill hollow in top of cake with remaining cherries and pile remaining cream on top. Grate remaining chocolate (from making cake) over cream.

BUTTERSCOTCH BUTTERFLIES

Preparation Time
20 minutes
Cooking Time
20 to 25 minutes
Makes
12 butterflies

These light, butterscotch-flavored cup-cakes are topped with a rich caramel cream. The same cake mixture can be baked in an 8-inch (20 cm) round cake pan, if you prefer. Bake it for about 35 minutes.

1 cup PLUS 2 tbsp	all-purpose flour	275 mL
1 tsp	baking soda	5 mL
1 cup	packed brown sugar	250 mL
1/2 cup	sour cream	125 mL
2	large eggs	2
1 tsp	vanilla extract	5 mL
1/2 cup	hot water	125 mL
Caramel Cream Filling:		
1/4 cup	granulated sugar	50 mL
1 tbsp	water	15 mL
1-1/2 cups	whipping cream	375 mL
1	can (10 oz/284 mL) mandarin oranges, well drained	1

1 Preheat oven to 350°F (180°C). Have ready a nonstick or lightly greased 12-cup muffin pan.

2 In a small bowl, sift together flour and baking soda. In a medium bowl, beat together sugar, cream, eggs and vanilla until smooth. With a metal spoon, fold in one-third of the flour mixture, followed by one-third of the hot water. Repeat until all flour mixture and water are used and a smooth, liquid batter is formed.

3 Spoon batter evenly into muffin pan, filling each cup about two-thirds full. Bake for 20 to 25 minutes or until well risen and cakes spring back when pressed gently. Let cool in pan for 5 minutes, then carefully turn out and let cool completely on a wire rack.

4 *Caramel Cream Filling:* In a small saucepan over medium heat, stir together sugar and water until sugar has dissolved. Increase heat and bring to boil. Boil for 2 minutes until honey-colored. Immediately remove from heat and quickly stir in 2 tbsp (25 mL) of the cream. Set aside.

5 In a medium bowl, whip remaining cream until it stands in soft peaks. With a metal spoon, carefully fold in caramel until well combined.

6 Cut a thin slice from top of each cake and cut each slice in half. Top each cake with some Caramel Cream Filling. Replace halved tops in filling at an angle to represent butterfly wings. Top each cake with three or four mandarin segments.

CREAMY STRAWBERRY TARTLETS

Preparation Time
15 minutes
Cooking Time
20 to 25 minutes
Makes
12 tartlets

These fruity tartlets are really easy to make. As they cook, the creamy topping cracks to reveal the strawberry filling. Serve them warm or let cool and top each with a dollop of whipped cream and half a strawberry.

1-1/4 cups	all-purpose flour	300 mL
Pinch	salt	Pinch
1/4 cup	shortening	50 mL
1/4 cup	margarine	50 mL
3 tbsp	cold water (approx)	45 mL
Filling:		
3 oz	cream cheese (at room temperature)	90 g
1/3 cup	whipping cream	75 mL
1 tbsp	granulated sugar	15 mL
1/2 tsp	almond extract	2 mL
1/3 cup	strawberry jam	75 mL

1 Preheat oven to 350°F (180°C). Have ready a nonstick or lightly greased 12-cup tartlet pan.

2 In a medium bowl, sift together flour and salt. With your fingertips or pastry blender, rub in shortening and margarine until mixture resembles fine crumbs. Add water and mix with a fork until mixture holds together (you may need a little extra water). Turn out onto a lightly floured surface and knead for a few seconds until smooth and free of cracks.

3 Roll out pastry to 1/4-inch (5 mm) thickness. With a 3-1/2-inch (9 cm) floured cookie cutter, cut out 12 rounds and use to line tartlet pan. Place a small ball of aluminum foil in each pastry shell and bake for 5 minutes. Remove foil and let shells cool slightly.

4 *Filling:* In a blender or food processor fitted with a metal blade, process cream cheese, cream, sugar and almond extract until smooth. (Alternatively, in a small bowl, beat all ingredients until smooth.)

5 Spoon equal amounts of strawberry jam into each pastry shell. Top with equal amounts of cream cheese mixture, filling just to top of pastry. Bake for 15 to 20 minutes or just until filling is set. Carefully remove tartlets from pan and let cool on a wire rack. Serve warm or cold.

Chocolate Truffle Cake

7

MUNCHIES IN MINUTES

Throwing a party these days almost requires taking out a second mortgage. The greater part of the cost, of course, is stocking the bar but there's not much I can do to help you there. This chapter *will* help, however, in the preparation of those essential savory nibbles that show you're the "hostess with the mostest".

Providing your guests with unusual and tasty munchies doesn't mean putting the rest of the family on bread and water for a week, nor does it require you to become a slave to the kitchen. All the recipes that follow are budget-conscious and most take just 10 to 15 minutes to prepare. Better still, all are delicious and easy to eat.

Whenever you see this symbol, *, it means that the recipe can be made ahead to this point, then covered and refrigerated for up to one day. Some of the savories, such as Spicy Cheese-Topped Crackers and Savory Choux Cups, require a little last-minute preparation.

Several of these scrumptious savory home-bakes lead double lives and, served in larger portions, make mouth-watering main courses. Try Savory Ham Slice, Ham and Watercress Strudel or Savory Choux Cups at your next dinner party.

CHEESY MUSTARD BITES

Preparation Time
10 minutes
Cooking Time
25 minutes
Makes
12 to 14 cookies

These cheese-flavored shortbread bites have a tangy filling of Dijon mustard. The rich, crumbly mouthfuls are best served slightly warm.

1 cup	all-purpose flour	250 mL
3 tbsp	semolina flour	45 mL
1/4 tsp	salt	1 mL
Pinch	cayenne pepper	Pinch
1/2 cup	butter	125 mL
1 cup	grated Cheddar cheese	250 mL
1/4 cup	milk	50 mL
1 tbsp	Dijon mustard	15 mL

1 Preheat oven to 350°F (180°C). Have ready a nonstick or lightly greased cookie sheet.

2 In a medium bowl, combine all-purpose and semolina flours, salt and cayenne. With your fingertips or pastry blender, rub in butter until mixture resembles fine crumbs. Stir in cheese. Add milk and, with a fork, stir until mixture holds together. Turn out dough onto a lightly floured surface and knead for 1 minute or until dough is smooth and free of cracks.

3 Divide dough in half and roll out each piece separately to 1/4-inch (5 mm) thickness. Spread one piece of dough with mustard and top with second piece of dough. Roll lightly to seal. With a floured 2-1/2-inch (6 cm) cookie cutter, cut out 12 to 14 rounds. Place on baking sheet and bake for 25 minutes or until lightly browned. Transfer to a wire rack and let cool.* If making ahead of time, reheat by arranging on a cookie sheet, covering with foil and heating in a 300°F (150°C) oven for 10 to 15 minutes.

FLUFFY SEAFOOD QUICHES

Preparation Time
20 minutes
Cooking Time
20 to 25 minutes
Makes
24 quiches

Filled with a mixture of shrimp and crab, these light mini-quiches are best served warm from the oven. For economy, you can use frozen artificial crabmeat — the flavor is excellent. Just thaw and chop it before using.

2-1/2 cups	all-purpose flour	625 mL
Pinch	salt	Pinch
1/2 cup	shortening	125 mL
1/2 cup	butter or margarine	125 mL
1/4 cup	cold water (approx)	50 mL
Filling:		
1	can (10 oz/284 mL) condensed cream of celery soup	1
3 oz	cooked shrimp, chopped	90 g
3 oz	cooked crabmeat, chopped	90 g
2	large eggs, separated (see Quick Tip, p. 129)	2
1/2 tsp	dried dill	2 mL
	Salt and freshly ground pepper	

1 Preheat oven to 400°F (200°C). Have ready two nonstick or lightly greased 12-cup tartlet pans.

2 In a medium bowl, sift together flour and salt. With your fingertips or pastry blender, rub in shortening and butter until mixture resembles fine crumbs. With a fork, gradually mix in enough water to form a stiff but not sticky dough.

3 Turn out dough onto a lightly floured surface and knead for a few seconds or until dough is smooth and free of cracks. Roll out to 1/4-inch (5 mm) thickness. With a 3-1/2-inch (9 cm) floured cookie cutter, cut out 24 rounds and use to line tartlet pans.

4 *Filling:* In a medium bowl, mix together soup, shrimp, crabmeat, egg yolks, dill, and salt and pepper to taste until ingredients are well combined.* In a separate medium bowl, whisk egg whites with a wire whisk or electric mixer until they stand in stiff peaks. With a metal spoon, carefully fold egg whites into seafood mixture until well combined.

5 Spoon equal amounts of filling into each pastry shell, filling just to top of pastry. Bake for 20 to 25 minutes or until well risen and golden. Carefully remove tartlets from pans and let cool slightly on a wire rack.

QUICK TIP

The speediest way to make shortcrust pastry for tartlets and quiches is to whip it up in a food processor, if you have one. Fit the processor with the metal blade and process the flour, salt, shortening and butter or margarine until the mixture resembles crumbs. With the processor running, slowly add the water in a steady stream until the mixture forms a ball.

Whether or not you have a food processor, it's a good idea to make large quantities of the rubbed-in flour and fat mixture. Simply omit the water from the pastry recipe and store the crumblike mixture in plastic bags. It will keep for several weeks in the refrigerator. Whenever you need pastry, measure out some of the mixture, add enough water to make a stiff dough, then roll out and use. As a rough guide, 1-3/4 cups (425 mL) rubbed-in mixture plus 2 to 3 tablespoons (25 to 45 mL) water makes enough pastry for 12 tartlets or one 7-inch (18 cm) quiche.

SOUR CREAM COOKIES WITH BLUE CHEESE

Preparation Time
15 minutes
Cooking Time
10 to 15 minutes
Makes
about 24 cookies

The delicious blue cheese topping in this recipe is one of my favorite "all-purpose" standbys. Not only is it wonderful spread on any savory cracker, but its sharp flavor goes well with barbecued steaks and fish — simply top with a dollop of the mixture just before serving. Diluted with whipping cream or milk, the same topping makes an excellent dip.

Cookies:

2 cups	**all-purpose flour**	**500 mL**
1/4 tsp	**salt**	**1 mL**
1 cup	**butter**	**250 mL**
2/3 cup	**sour cream**	**150 mL**

Topping:

4 oz	**Roquefort cheese (or other blue cheese)**	**125 g**
1/4 cup	**butter (at room temperature)**	**50 mL**
1 tbsp	**whisky or brandy**	**15 mL**
	Freshly ground pepper	
	Paprika for garnish	

1 Preheat oven to 375°F (190°C). Have ready two nonstick or lightly greased cookie sheets.

2 *Cookies:* In a medium bowl, sift together flour and salt. With your fingertips or pastry blender, rub in butter until mixture resembles fine crumbs. With a fork, mix in sour cream until mixture clings together.

3 Turn out dough onto a lightly floured surface and knead for a few seconds or until dough is smooth and free of cracks. Roll out to 1/4-inch (5 mm) thickness. With a 2-1/2-inch (6 cm) floured cookie cutter, cut out about 24 rounds. Place about 2 inches (5 cm) apart on cookie sheets and bake for 10 to 15 minutes or until golden brown. Carefully remove from cookie sheets and let cool completely on a wire rack.

4 *Topping:* In a medium bowl, mash together cheese and butter with a fork until smooth. Stir in whisky and season to taste with pepper.* Just before serving, spread a little of the cheese mixture on each cookie and sprinkle with a little paprika for garnish.

SAVORY CHOUX CUPS

Preparation Time
20 minutes
Cooking Time
20 to 25 minutes
Makes
36 to 40 puffs

Versatile choux pastry can hold a luscious sweet filling (see Strawberry Puff, p. 86) or, as here, a tasty savory one. If you make the choux cups a little larger (use a tablespoon instead of a teaspoon for shaping the uncooked pastry), the filled cups make a deliciously light main course.

Pastry:

Choux Pastry dough (see Strawberry Puff, p. 86).

Chicken Filling:

1 cup	chopped cooked chicken	250 mL
1 cup	mayonnaise	250 mL
1/4 cup	mango chutney or other sweet chutney	50 mL
1 tbsp	tomato paste	15 mL
1/2 tsp	garam masala (see Back to Basics, p. 15) OR	2 mL
1/4 tsp	curry powder	1 mL
	Salt and freshly ground pepper	
	Poppyseeds for garnish	

Pâté Filling:

4 oz	cream cheese	125 g
4 oz	smooth liver pâté	125 g
	Whipping cream	
	Salt and freshly ground pepper	
	Parsley sprigs for garnish	

1 Preheat oven to 400°F (200°C). Have ready two nonstick or lightly greased cookie sheets.

2 Drop choux pastry by teaspoonfuls, about 2 inches (5 cm) apart, onto cookie sheets, making 18 to 20 even-sized heaps. Bake for 20 to 25 minutes until well risen and golden brown. Remove from cookie sheets and let cool completely on a wire rack.

3 *Chicken Filling:* In a medium bowl, mix together chicken, mayonnaise, chutney, tomato paste and garam masala. Season to taste with salt and pepper and set aside.

4 *Pâté Filling:* In separate bowl, mix together cream cheese and liver pâté. Mix in enough cream to give a spreading consistency. Season to taste with salt and pepper.*

5 With a sharp knife, carefully cut choux balls in half horizontally. With a small spoon, scoop out and discard any soft dough from each half to make room for fillings. Invert top halves of choux balls and trim bases, if necessary, so they stand level. Just before serving, fill half of the choux cups with Chicken Filling and sprinkle each with poppyseeds. Fill remaining cups with Pâté Filling and garnish with parsley sprigs.

QUICK TIP

A speedy lunch or supper dish for four to six people can be made by adding 1/2 cup (125 mL) grated Cheddar cheese to the choux pastry mixture (see Strawberry Puff, p. 86) after adding the eggs. Spoon the paste into a ring on a nonstick or lightly greased cookie sheet. Bake in oven at 400°F (200°C) for 40 minutes or until well risen and golden brown. Serve hot, as is, with soup and a salad, or fill the center with cooked seafood, chicken or ham in a white sauce.

ANCHOVY CHEESE TWISTS

Preparation Time
15 minutes

Cooking Time
10 minutes

Makes
about 16 twists

Even if anchovies are not one of your favorite pizza toppings, you're sure to enjoy these savory cheese snacks. The usually strong-tasting fish are first soaked in milk to give them a pleasant, mild flavor that teams well with the cheesy pastry.

1	can (1.75 oz/50 g) anchovy fillets, drained	1
	Milk	
1 cup	all-purpose flour	250 mL
Pinch	each salt and cayenne pepper	Pinch
1/3 cup	butter or margarine	75 mL
1/2 cup	grated Cheddar cheese	125 mL
1	egg yolk (see Quick Tip, p.118)	1
	Cold water	

1 Preheat oven to 425°F (220°C). Have ready two nonstick or lightly greased cookie sheets.

2 Place anchovy fillets in a shallow dish. Pour enough milk over to cover and set aside to soak.

3 In a medium bowl, sift together flour, salt and cayenne. With your fingertips or pastry blender, rub in butter until mixture resembles fine crumbs. Stir in cheese. With a fork, mix in egg yolk and enough water to form a stiff dough.

4 Turn out dough onto a lightly floured surface and knead for a few seconds or until dough is smooth and free of cracks. Roll out to a 12- × 9-inch (30 × 23 cm) rectangle and trim edges. Cut in half to make two 9- × 6-inch (23 × 15 cm) rectangles. Cut each rectangle into about eight 6-inch (15 cm) long strips.

5 Drain milk from anchovies and pat dry with paper towels. Cut each fillet in half lengthwise. Place half a fillet on each strip of pastry. Carefully lift each strip onto cookie sheet, twisting both ends in opposite directions to make a twist.

6 Bake for 10 minutes until golden brown. Carefully transfer to a wire rack and let cool completely.*

STUFFED DEVILS

Preparation Time
10 minutes
Cooking Time
10 minutes
Makes
20 hors d'oeuvres

These speedy savories are a variation on an old British recipe with the curious name "Devils on Horseback". Stuffed Devils are quick to prepare and make excellent finger food to serve at parties.

20	whole salted peanuts	20
20	pimento-stuffed green olives	20
20	large prunes, pitted	20
10	slices bacon	10
20	toothpicks	20

1 Preheat oven to 400°F (200°C). Have ready a cookie sheet. Carefully stuff peanuts inside olives, then insert each olive into a pitted prune. Stretch bacon slices by laying each slice on a chopping board and running the back of a knife along the slice. Cut each slice in half crosswise and roll each half around a stuffed prune. Secure each with a toothpick.* Arrange on cookie sheet and bake for 10 minutes. Drain well on paper towels and serve hot.

SPICY CHEESE-TOPPED CRACKERS

Preparation Time
15 minutes
Cooking Time
15 to 20 minutes
Makes
about 15 crackers

These tangy crackers are topped with savory cheese mixture, then served sizzling straight from the broiler. If you prefer, brush the pastry with beaten egg before baking and omit the topping. This plain version is great with dips and pâté.

Crackers:

1-1/3 cups	all-purpose flour	325 mL
1/2 cup	butter or margarine (at room temperature)	125 mL
1	large egg	1
2 tsp	baking powder	10 mL
1/4 tsp	salt	1 mL
1/4 tsp	ground cumin	1 mL
Pinch	ground ginger	Pinch
Pinch	cayenne pepper	Pinch

Topping:

3/4 cup	grated Cheddar cheese	175 mL
1/2 cup	pitted chopped black olives (about 25 whole)	125 mL
1/4 cup	finely chopped green onions	50 mL
1/4 cup	mayonnaise	50 mL

1 Preheat oven to 375°F (190°C). Have ready two nonstick or lightly greased cookie sheets.

2 *Crackers:* In a medium bowl and using an electric mixer, beat together all ingredients for Crackers until well combined. Gather mixture into a ball and turn out onto a lightly floured surface. Knead for a few seconds or until smooth and free of cracks.

3 Roll out pastry to 1/4-inch (5 mm) thickness. With a 2-1/2-inch (6 cm) floured cookie cutter, cut out about 15 rounds and arrange, about 2 inches (5 cm) apart, on cookie sheets. Bake for 15 to 20 minutes or until golden brown. Remove from cookie sheets and let cool completely on a wire rack.

4 *Topping:* In a small bowl, mix together all ingredients for Topping until well combined. * Just before serving, arrange Crackers on rack in broiler pan. Spoon equal amounts of Topping over each Cracker and broil for 1 to 2 minutes or until Topping bubbles.

HAM AND WATERCRESS STRUDEL

Preparation Time
20 minutes
Cooking Time
30 to 35 minutes
Makes
one 10-inch (25 cm) strudel, 8 to 10 servings

This light strudel uses wafer-thin sheets of phyllo pastry to enclose the savory filling. Phyllo is a pastry traditionally used to make the deliciously sticky cakes for which Greece is famous. Read the Quick Tip on p. 112 if this is your first time baking with phyllo.

1 cup	finely chopped watercress (about half a bunch)	250 mL
1/2 cup	chopped cooked ham	125 mL
1/2 cup	cottage cheese	125 mL
2	finely chopped green onions	2
	Salt and freshly ground pepper	
6	sheets phyllo pastry (about 6 oz/180 g) (see Quick Tip, p.112)	6
1/2 cup	butter, melted	125 mL
1/2 cup	crushed cornflakes	125 mL
1 tbsp	Dijon mustard	15 mL

1 Preheat oven to 375°F (190°C). Have ready a nonstick or lightly greased cookie sheet.

2 In a medium bowl, mix together watercress, ham, cottage cheese and green onions. Season to taste with salt and pepper. Set aside.

3 Working quickly, lay one sheet phyllo pastry on a clean surface with one short end nearest you. Keep remaining sheets of pastry covered with a damp tea towel (see Quick Tip, p. 112). Using pastry brush, lightly brush phyllo with some of the melted butter and sprinkle with about 2 tbsp (25 mL) crushed cornflakes. Repeat with next four sheets pastry. Top with remaining sixth sheet and spread evenly with mustard.

4 Spoon ham and watercress mixture in a strip along short end of pastry nearest you, leaving a 1-1/2-inch (4 cm) border on short end and on two sides. Fold in long sides of pastry 1-1/2 inches (4 cm), then roll up pastry like a jelly roll, starting at the short end nearest you.

5 Carefully place roll seam side down, on cookie sheet. Brush all over with remaining butter. Bake for 30 to 35 minutes or until golden brown. Carefully remove strudel from cookie sheet and let cool completely on a wire rack.* Cut in slices with a serrated knife to serve.

QUICK TIP

Most phyllo pastry is sold frozen so follow the instructions on the package for thawing. Generally, you need to thaw the whole package in the refrigerator overnight, remove the pastry you require, and re-freeze the sheets remaining in the package.

Since phyllo pastry is so thin, once thawed and exposed to the air it dries out very quickly and becomes brittle and unusable. For any recipe using phyllo pastry, assemble and prepare all the other ingredients first, then have ready two clean damp tea towels. Remove the required number of phyllo pastry sheets from the package, spread out the pile on one tea towel and cover the stack with the other towel. Each time you remove a sheet of pastry from the pile, re-cover the remaining pastry with the damp tea towel.

Work as quickly and as carefully as you can on an unfloured surface. Once you've assembled the recipe and it's safely in the oven, you can breathe a sigh of relief — the results will be well worth the effort!

MUSHROOM TOASTS

Preparation Time
10 minutes
Cooking Time
20 minutes
Makes
12 toasts

One of the simplest savories, these crisp bread rounds are topped with a garlicky mushroom mixture and sour cream. They're very quickly prepared but must be served piping hot from the oven.

1/2 cup	butter	125 mL
6	large slices whole wheat bread	6
2 cups	chopped mushrooms	500 mL
1/2 cup	chopped fresh parsley	125 mL
1	small clove garlic, crushed	1
	Salt and freshly ground pepper	
1/3 cup	sour cream	75 mL
	Grated Parmesan cheese for garnish	

1 Preheat oven to 400°F (200°C). Have ready a 12-cup tartlet pan.

2 In a small saucepan over medium heat, melt butter. With a 2-1/2-inch (6 cm) cookie cutter, cut two rounds from each slice of bread, avoiding crusts. (Keep trimmings to make into bread crumbs and use in another recipe.) Using a pastry brush, brush bread rounds on both sides with some of the butter. Place a bread round in each cup of tartlet pan. Bake for 10 minutes or until golden and crisp.

3 Meanwhile, reheat remaining melted butter over medium-high heat and sauté mushrooms, parsley and garlic for 3 to 5 minutes or until mushrooms are softened. Drain any excess moisture from pan. Season to taste with salt and pepper.*

4 Spoon equal amounts of mushroom mixture onto each bread round. Top with equal amounts of sour cream and sprinkle with Parmesan cheese. Return to oven and bake for 10 minutes.

SAVORY HAM SLICES

Preparation Time
15 minutes
Cooking Time
30 to 35 minutes
Makes
32 hors d'oeuvres

In this recipe, a base of relish- or chutney-topped pastry is covered with a light ham and egg mixture. Serve in small squares for a party snack or in larger slices, with a salad, for a main course. I use tomato chutney for this recipe, but you can use your own favorite relish or chutney.

Pastry:

1-1/4 cups	all-purpose flour	300 mL
Pinch	salt	Pinch
1/4 cup	shortening	50 mL
1/4 cup	margarine	50 mL
3 tbsp	cold water (approx)	45 mL

Topping:

1/2 cup	tomato chutney	125 mL
1/2 cup	all-purpose flour	125 mL
1/2 cup	milk	125 mL
1/4 cup	butter or margarine (at room temperature)	50 mL
2	large eggs, separated (see Quick Tip, p. 129)	2
2 tbsp	grated Parmesan cheese	25 mL
1 tsp	powdered mustard	5 mL
	Salt and freshly ground pepper	
1/2 cup	chopped cooked ham	125 mL

1 Preheat oven to 400°F (200°C). Have ready a nonstick or lightly greased 11- × 7-inch (28 × 18 cm) cake pan.

2 *Pastry:* In a medium bowl, sift together flour and salt. With your fingertips or pastry blender, rub in shortening and margarine until mixture resembles fine crumbs. With a fork, gradually mix in enough water to form a stiff dough.

3 Turn out dough onto a lightly floured surface and knead for 1 minute or until dough is smooth and free of cracks. Roll out to an 11-1/2 × 7-1/2-inch (29 × 19 cm) rectangle and use to line base and partway up sides of pan.

4 *Topping:* Spread chutney evenly over Pastry and set aside. In a medium bowl, beat together flour, milk, butter, egg yolks, Parmesan, mustard, and salt and pepper to taste until smooth. Stir in ham.

5 In a separate medium bowl, whisk egg whites with a wire whisk or electric mixer until they stand in stiff peaks. With a metal spoon, carefully fold egg whites into ham mixture until well combined. Spoon mixture evenly over chutney, spreading right to edges of pan.

6 Bake for 30 to 35 minutes until golden and well risen. Let cool in pan.* Serve warm or cold, cut into squares.

Lemon and Cherry Tea Biscuits

8

BAKES
FROM
ABROAD

Come with me on a gastronomic grand tour as we sample some delicious cakes and pastries from around the world. We'll visit such far-flung destinations as the West Indies and Denmark to discover how our friends and neighbors overseas spend their baking day.

I've made a collection of traditional home-bakes and adapted the recipes so you can enjoy them too. You won't need to search for unusual ingredients in specialty stores —your local supermarket should stock everything you need. These are homey country-style recipes reflecting each land's unique fare. They're all easy to make and will add an international flavor to *your* baking day.

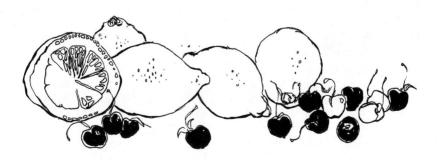

SWISS CHERRY TORTE

Preparation Time
10 minutes
Cooking Time
35 to 40 minutes
Makes
one 8-inch (20 cm) round torte

Serve this luscious cherry dessert in small wedges with cream or chocolate ice cream.

1 cup	plain sweet cookie crumbs (8 to 10 cookies)	250 mL
1/2 cup	ground almonds	125 mL
1/3 cup	granulated sugar	75 mL
1/2 cup	whipping cream	125 mL
4	egg yolks (see Quick Tip, p. 118)	4
1/3 cup	butter (at room temperature)	75 mL
1	lemon, grated rind	1
1	can (14 oz/398 mL) pitted cherries, drained	1
	Whipped cream and grated chocolate for decoration	

1 Preheat oven to 350°F (180°C). Have ready a nonstick or lightly greased 8-inch (20 cm) round cake pan.

2 In a medium bowl, beat together cookie crumbs, almonds, sugar, cream, egg yolks, butter and lemon rind until creamy. Spoon one-third of the mixture evenly over base of cake pan. Bake for about 5 minutes or until golden brown.

3 Top cooked base evenly with cherries. Spoon remaining egg yolk mixture evenly over top, smoothing surface. Return to oven and bake for 30 to 35 minutes longer or until golden and firm. Let cool completely in cake pan. Transfer to a serving plate and decorate with whipped cream and grated chocolate.

QUICK TIP

If a recipe calls for only egg yolks, there's no need to waste the whites. Treat the family to meringues for dessert.

For every 3 egg whites you'll need a pinch of cream of tartar and 3/4 cup (175 mL) granulated sugar. In a clean, grease-free bowl, whisk egg whites and cream of tartar with a wire whisk or electric mixer until standing in stiff peaks. Add half of the sugar and continue whisking until sugar has dissolved and mixture is stiff and shiny. (If you rub a little of the mixture between your finger and thumb, it should feel smooth, not grainy.) With a metal spoon, fold in remaining sugar.

Line a cookie sheet with waxed paper. Spoon or, using an icing bag fitted with large star tip, pipe meringue in even-sized heaps onto cookie sheet. Bake in a 250°F (120°C) oven for about 1 hour. Turn off oven and leave meringues in oven to dry out for 1-1/2 to 2 hours longer or until dry and brittle. When cold, remove from oven and sandwich together in pairs with whipped cream.

RICOTTA CHEESECAKE

Preparation Time
10 minutes
Cooking Time
40 to 50 minutes
Makes
one 8-inch (20 cm) cheesecake, 6 servings

Ricotta, a soft, white curd cheese, is used widely in Italian cooking. Its creamy texture and mild flavor make this cheesecake from Tuscany deliciously rich.

1/2 cup	ground almonds	125 mL
1 lb	ricotta cheese	500 g
1/2 cup	granulated sugar	125 mL
2	egg yolks (see Quick Tip, p. 118)	2
1	large lemon, grated rind and juice	1
3/4 cup	sultana raisins	175 mL

1 Preheat oven to 375°F (190°C). Lightly grease an 8-inch (20 cm) round cake pan. Sprinkle base and sides of pan with ground almonds, tilting and shaking pan to coat evenly.

2 In a food processor fitted with a metal blade, process cheese, sugar, egg yolks, lemon rind and juice until smooth. Pour into a medium bowl, add sultana raisins and stir well. (Alternatively, press cheese through a sieve into a medium bowl and beat in remaining ingredients.)

3 Pour cheese mixture into cake pan and smooth surface. Bake for 40 to 50 minutes or until golden brown and set. Turn off oven, open door and let cheesecake cool in oven. Chill in refrigerator, then cut into wedges to serve.

COCONUT BREAD

Preparation Time
10 minutes
Cooking Time
35 to 40 minutes
Makes
one loaf

A great favorite in the West Indies, this quick bread is delicious when sliced and buttered. It is traditionally made with fresh grated coconut and coconut milk; however, this simpler version uses shredded coconut and canned coconut milk. If you can't find coconut milk in your local supermarket, canned pina colada mix makes a good substitute.

1/3 cup	shortening	75 mL
1-1/2 cups	all-purpose flour	375 mL
1 tbsp	baking powder	15 mL
1/4 tsp	salt	1 mL
1/2 cup	granulated sugar	125 mL
1/2 cup	unsweetened shredded coconut	125 mL
2/3 cup	coconut milk	150 mL
1	large egg	1
1/2 tsp	vanilla extract	2 mL
	Granulated sugar	

1 Preheat oven to 375°F (190°C). Have ready a nonstick or lightly greased 7-1/2- × 3-1/2-inch (3 cup/750 mL) loaf pan.

2 In a small saucepan over medium heat, melt shortening. Remove pan from heat and set aside to cool.

3 In a medium bowl, sift together flour, baking powder and salt. Stir in 1/2 cup (125 mL) sugar and shredded coconut, and set aside.
In a small bowl, beat together coconut milk, egg and vanilla until well combined.

4 Add coconut milk mixture and melted shortening to dry ingredients and mix well with a fork until well combined. Spoon mixture into loaf pan and smooth surface. Sprinkle evenly with a little sugar. Bake for 35 to 40 minutes or until golden and well risen and skewer inserted in center comes out clean. Let cool in pan for 5 minutes, then turn out and let cool completely on a wire rack.

BRANDY SNAPS

Preparation Time
20 minutes
Cooking Time
10 minutes
Makes
about 12 brandy snaps

No posh English party would be complete without a plate piled high with these crisp, cream-filled cookies. The name dates from the time when they were flavored with brandy instead of lemon juice. The cookies are baked four or five at a time. Then, while still soft from the oven, they are molded around the handle of a wooden spoon to form tube shapes.

1/3 cup	granulated sugar	75 mL
1/3 cup	corn syrup	75 mL
1/3 cup	butter or margarine	75 mL
1 tsp	lemon juice	5 mL
2/3 cup	all-purpose flour	150 mL
1 tsp	ground ginger	5 mL
2/3 cup	whipping cream	150 mL

1 Preheat oven to 350°F (180°C). Have ready a nonstick or lightly greased large cookie sheet. Lightly grease the handle of a wooden spoon and set aside.

2 In a small saucepan over medium heat, mix together sugar, syrup, butter and lemon juice until butter and sugar have dissolved. Remove pan from heat. Sift in flour and ginger and beat until smooth. Drop four or five rounded teaspoonfuls of the mixture at a time, about 4 inches (10 cm) apart, onto cookie sheet. Bake for 10 minutes or until golden and lacy-looking.

3 As soon as cookies are baked, carefully remove each one with a spatula and mold around wooden spoon handle to form a tube. Slide off spoon and let cool on a wire rack. (If the cookies become too brittle to shape, return cookie sheet to oven for 1 minute until they soften slightly.) Repeat baking and molding with remaining mixture.

4 Shortly before serving, whip cream until it stands in soft peaks. Spoon or, using icing bag, pipe a little cream into both ends of each Brandy Snap. Pile on a plate and serve.

CLAFOUTI

Preparation Time
10 minutes
Cooking Time
45 minutes
Makes
*one 8-inch (20 cm) flan,
6 to 8 servings*

The Limousin area of France is cherry-growing country and this simple flan is traditionally made at harvest time with the local fruit. I've given it a Canadian twist and added our national favorite — blueberries.

1/2 cup	all-purpose flour	125 mL
1/3 cup	granulated sugar	75 mL
1-1/4 cups	milk	300 mL
2	large eggs	2
2 tbsp	butter, melted	25 mL
1 tbsp	brandy (optional)	15 mL
1 tsp	vanilla extract	5 mL
2 cups	blueberries (fresh or frozen and thawed)	500 mL
	Whipped cream	

1 Preheat oven to 400°F (200°C). Have ready a nonstick or lightly greased 8-inch (20 cm) pie plate.

2 In a medium bowl, beat together flour, sugar, milk, eggs, butter, brandy and vanilla until smooth and creamy. Pour 3/4 cup (175 mL) of batter into pie plate and bake for 5 minutes or until set.

3 Spread blueberries evenly over cooked batter. Pour remaining batter over blueberries. Bake for 20 minutes, then reduce oven temperature to 375°F (190°C). Bake for 20 minutes longer or until golden and well risen and skewer inserted in center comes out clean. Let cool slightly in plate (the flan will sink a little) and serve warm with whipped cream.

FETA CHEESE PIE

Preparation Time
15 minutes
Cooking Time
40 to 45 minutes
Makes
*one 11- × 7-inch
(28 × 18 cm) pie*

Some years ago, I spent an idyllic vacation in a tiny Greek village. Each morning we would visit the local bakery where we bought freshly baked cheese pies to munch on while strolling to the beach. They taste as good today and still remind me of that seemingly endless summer.

8	sheets phyllo pastry (about 8 oz/250 g), thawed (see Quick Tip, p. 112)	8
3/4 lb	feta cheese	375 g
3	large eggs	3
Pinch	grated nutmeg	Pinch
	Freshly ground pepper	
1/3 cup	butter, melted	75 mL

1 Preheat oven to 375°F (190°C). Have ready an 11- × 7-inch (28 × 18 cm) cake pan.

2 In a medium bowl, mash feta cheese with a fork. Beat in eggs, nutmeg and pepper to taste.

3 Using pastry brush, lightly brush cake pan with some of the melted butter. Fold one sheet of phyllo pastry in half and use to line base of cake pan. Brush with some of the melted butter. Repeat with two more sheets of pastry. Spoon over half of the feta cheese mixture. Top with fourth sheet of pastry and brush with some of the butter. Repeat process, with two more sheets of pastry, then spoon over remaining feta cheese mixture. Finally, top with remaining two sheets of pastry, brushing each with remaining melted butter.

4 With a sharp knife, score pie into 12 squares. Bake for 40 to 45 minutes until golden brown. Let cool slightly in pan, then cut into squares and serve warm.

BAKEWELL TART

Preparation Time
15 minutes
Cooking Time
45 minutes
Makes
one 8-inch (20 cm) tart,
6 to 8 servings

This almond-flavored tart, sometimes called Bakewell Pudding, originated in the picturesque town of Bakewell in the north of England. Traditionally, the tart was made with puff pastry, but this version, using shortcrust, is more common today.

Pastry:

1-1/4 cups	all-purpose flour	300 mL
Pinch	salt	Pinch
1/4 cup	butter or margarine	50 mL
1/4 cup	shortening	50 mL
3 tbsp	cold water (approx)	45 mL

Filling:

1/2 cup	granulated sugar	125 mL
1/2 cup	butter (at room temperature)	125 mL
3	large eggs, separated (see Quick Tip, p. 129)	3
1 tsp	almond extract	5 mL
3/4 cup	ground almonds	175 mL
1/2 cup	strawberry jam	125 mL

1 Preheat oven to 375°F (190°C). Have ready a nonstick or lightly greased 8-3/4-inch (22 cm) pie plate.

2 *Pastry:* In a medium bowl, sift together flour and salt. With your fingertips or pastry blender, rub in butter and shortening until mixture resembles fine crumbs. With a fork, gradually mix in water to form a stiff dough.

3 Turn out dough onto a lightly floured surface and knead for a few seconds or until dough is smooth and free of cracks. Roll out to 1/4-inch (5 mm) thickness and use to line base and sides of pie plate. Line pastry with foil, weigh down with weights and bake "blind" (see Quick Tip, p.125) for 15 minutes. Remove weights and foil.

4 *Filling:* In a medium bowl, beat together sugar, butter, egg yolks and almond extract until pale yellow and fluffy. Stir in ground almonds.

5 In a separate medium bowl, whisk egg whites with a wire whisk or electric mixer until they stand in stiff peaks. With a metal spoon, carefully fold egg whites into almond mixture until ingredients are well combined.

6 Spread strawberry jam evenly over pastry. Spoon egg white mixture evenly over jam, spreading to edges of pie plate. Bake for about 30 minutes or until golden brown and risen. Let cool in pie plate and serve warm or cold.

QUICK TIP

Some tart and quiche recipes instruct you to bake the pastry case "blind" before adding the filling. This doesn't mean you must don an eye mask and grope around the kitchen!

To bake "blind", line a tart or quiche pan with pastry. Cut a circle of aluminum foil slightly larger than the pan and place over pastry. Cover foil with an even layer of uncooked rice or pasta shapes, dried beans or ceramic baking beans. This weighs the pastry down and keeps it flat during baking. Bake in a 375°F (190°C) oven to 15 minutes. Remove foil and weights before adding filling.

This partial baking of the pastry shell prevents it from going soggy once the filling is added.

DANISH APPLE CAKE

Preparation Time
20 minutes
Cooking Time
40 to 45 minutes
Makes
one 8-inch (20 cm) round "cake", 6 servings

This "cake" is really a deep-dish apple pie made, Scandinavian-style, with a crunchy, nutty topping. Do use butter for the pastry—the rich flavor is well worth the extra expense.

Pastry:

2 cups	all-purpose flour	500 mL
2/3 cup	granulated sugar	150 mL
1/2 tsp	salt	2 mL
1/2 cup	butter	125 mL
1/2 cup	shortening	125 mL
1	large egg, beaten	1

Filling:

4	Granny Smith apples, peeled, cored and sliced	4
1/3 cup	granulated sugar	75 mL
1/3 cup	sultana raisins	75 mL
1/3 cup	chopped walnuts	75 mL

Topping:

1/2 cup	granulated sugar	125 mL
1/2 cup	butter	125 mL
1/3 cup	chopped walnuts	75 mL

1 Preheat oven to 400°F (200°C). Have ready a nonstick or lightly greased 8-inch (20 cm) round cake pan.

2 *Pastry:* In a food processor fitted with a metal blade, process flour, sugar, salt, butter and shortening until mixture resembles fine crumbs. With machine running, add egg and process until mixture forms a ball. (Alternatively, in a medium bowl, sift together flour and salt. With your fingertips or pastry blender, rub in butter and shortening until mixture resembles fine crumbs. Stir in sugar. Add egg and, with a fork, mix to a stiff dough.)

3 Turn out dough onto a lightly floured surface and gather into a ball. Divide dough in half. Roll out one half to an 8-inch (20 cm) circle and place on base of cake pan. Carefully press dough evenly over base and up sides of cake pan. With your thumbs, gently ease sides up and over top edge of pan. Refrigerate for 15 minutes.

4 *Filling:* In a large bowl, mix together apples, sugar, sultana raisins and walnuts. Mound Filling in pastry-lined cake pan. Roll out remaining pastry to a circle large enough to cover Filling. Place over Filling, dampening and sealing edges well. (The pastry will be very crumbly and may fall to bits. Just patch it carefully — it may look messy but won't show once you've added the topping.)

5 *Topping:* In a food processor fitted with a metal blade, process sugar, butter and walnuts until well combined. (Alternatively, in a medium bowl, beat together sugar and butter. Finely chop walnuts and stir in.) Spoon Topping evenly over pastry lid.

6 Place cake pan on a large cookie sheet. Bake for 20 minutes, then cover with a sheet of aluminum foil. Bake for 20 to 25 minutes longer or until top is golden and crusty. Let cool in pan and serve warm or cold.

JANHAGEL

Preparation Time
10 minutes
Cooking Time
35 to 40 minutes
Makes
about 20 bars

This rich, spicy cinnamon shortbread from Holland has a lovely, nutty topping. Cut it into 1-inch (2.5 cm) bars and serve with coffee or to accompany ice cream.

1 cup	butter (at room temperature)	250 mL
2/3 cup	granulated sugar	150 mL
1-1/2 cups	all-purpose flour	375 mL
1 tsp	ground cinnamon	5 mL
1	egg yolk, beaten (see Quick Tip, p.118)	1
1/3 cup	chopped mixed unsalted nuts	75 mL

1 Preheat oven to 325°F (160°C). Have ready a nonstick or lightly greased 11- × 7-inch (28 × 18 cm) cake pan.

2 In a medium bowl, cream together butter and sugar until pale yellow and fluffy. Sift in flour and cinnamon and mix with your hands or a pastry blender until mixture is crumbly.

3 Press mixture evenly onto base of cake pan with palms of your hands. Prick all over with a fork. Pour egg yolk over mixture and spread evenly with a pastry brush. Sprinkle with chopped nuts. Bake for 35 to 40 minutes or until golden. Let cool in cake pan, then cut into bars.

GLAZED ORANGE CAKE

Preparation Time
15 minutes
Cooking Time
30 to 35 minutes
Makes
one 8-inch (20 cm)
round cake

The Portuguese satisfy their sweet tooth with this light citrus cake and its popularity has spread across the Atlantic.

3/4 cup	granulated sugar	175 mL
3/4 cup	butter or margarine (at room temperature)	175 mL
3	large eggs	3
1 cup	all-purpose flour	250 mL
1 tsp	baking powder	5 mL
1	medium orange, grated rind and juice	1
Glaze:		
2 tbsp	liquid honey	25 mL
2 tbsp	orange juice	25 mL

1 Preheat oven to 350°F (180°C). Have ready a nonstick or lightly greased 8-inch (20 cm) round cake pan.

2 In a medium bowl, beat together sugar, butter and eggs until pale yellow and fluffy. In a small bowl, sift together flour and baking powder.

3 With a metal spoon, fold flour mixture, then orange rind and juice into butter mixture. (The mixture may look curdled.) Spoon batter into cake pan and smooth surface. Bake for 30 to 35 minutes or until cake shrinks away from side of pan, top springs back when pressed gently and skewer inserted in center comes out clean. Let cool in pan for 5 minutes, then turn out onto wire rack.

4 *Glaze:* In a small saucepan over medium heat, heat honey and orange juice. Place plate under wire rack holding cake. With a toothpick, prick top of cake all over and carefully pour honey mixture over cake. Let cool completely.

Separating egg yolks from their whites can be tricky, but with a bit of practice you can do it the professional way. Crack the egg over a bowl and divide the shell in half. Using the two halves of shell like little cups, hold them over the bowl. Carefully transfer the yolk back and forth, from one cup to the other, making sure the yolk does not break, and letting the white fall into the bowl.

An even easier way to separate an egg is to crack it onto a saucer. Carefully invert an egg cup over the yolk to cover it completely. Holding the egg cup to the saucer, just pour off the white into a bowl, leaving the yolk safe and sound under the egg cup.

Tabby Cat Cake

9

KIDS' STUFF

Want to ensure your child's next party is a resounding success? With a cake shaped like a favorite teddy bear as a centerpiece, you can't lose. Or why not treat a wild-West fan to a fort, or throw a pirate party with a delicious edible treasure chest as the centerpiece. If all these novelty cakes sound as if they're way out of your league, look again.

If you can make a simple sponge cake and whip up a bowl or two of frosting, give these cakes a try. You'll be surprised how easy they are. The basic recipes are good and fast, although you'll need to spend a few extra minutes decorating the finished cakes. This doesn't mean you need a master's degree in Icing Bag Technology, you simply have to work some magic with a few candies, licorice shoelaces and cake decorations.

What's important is to have fun. Once you've tried a few of these ideas, experiment and create a unique cake for *your* birthday girl or boy.

TABBY CAT CAKE

Preparation Time
35 minutes
Cooking Time
25 to 30 minutes
Makes
one 8-inch (20 cm)
round cake

Who could resist this striped pussycat with its crunchy cornflake coating? When adding the chocolate stripes to the cat's face, use a teaspoon to trickle the sprinkles onto the buttercream so they go exactly where you want.

Cake:

3/4 cup	granulated sugar	175 mL
1/3 cup	butter or margarine (at room temperature)	75 mL
2	large eggs	2
1	orange, grated rind	1
1-1/2 cups	all-purpose flour	375 mL
2 tsp	baking powder	10 mL
1/4 tsp	salt	1 mL
1/2 cup	milk	125 mL

Buttercream:

3 cups	sifted icing sugar	750 mL
1/2 cup	butter (at room temperature)	125 mL
3 tbsp	milk (approx)	45 mL
	Yellow and red food coloring	

Decoration:

2 oz	semi-sweet chocolate, melted and cooled (see Quick Tip, p.141,61)	60 g
1 cup	cornflakes (approx)	250 mL
1/4 cup	chocolate sprinkles	50 mL
2	Smarties candies (for eyes)	2

1 Preheat oven to 350°F (180°C). Have ready a nonstick or lightly greased 8-inch (20 cm) round cake pan.

2 *Cake:* In a medium bowl, beat together sugar and butter until pale yellow and fluffy. Add eggs, one at a time, beating well after each addition. Stir in orange rind.

3 In a separate medium bowl, sift together flour, baking powder and salt. With a metal spoon, carefully fold one-third of the flour mixture, followed by one-third of the milk into creamed mixture. Repeat until all flour mixture and milk are used and a smooth batter is formed.

4 Spoon mixture into cake pan and smooth surface. Bake for 25 to 30 minutes or until cake shrinks away from sides of pan, top springs back when gently pressed, and skewer inserted in center comes out clean. Let cool in pan for 5 minutes, then turn out and let cool completely on a wire rack.

5 *Buttercream:* In a medium bowl, beat together icing sugar, butter and enough milk to give a spreading consistency. Beat in enough food coloring to tint Buttercream orange.

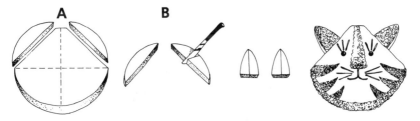

6 *Decoration:* In a small bowl over a saucepan of gently simmering water or in top of double boiler, melt chocolate, stirring occasionally until smooth. Remove from heat and set aside to cool.

7 Score a cross on top of the cake to divide it into four equal segments. Cut two semi-circles as shown in diagram A from upper two segments of cake. Cut each semi-circle in half as in diagram B and sandwich the halves together with some of the Buttercream to make two cat's ear shapes. Spread top and sides of ears with more Buttercream and coat evenly with cornflakes. Set aside.

8 Spread top and sides of rest of cake with remaining Buttercream and stick ears in place. Coat sides of cake with cornflakes and arrange a triangle of cornflakes down center of face to represent cat's nose.

9 With a sharp knife, lightly draw through Buttercream to mark stripes on top of cake from nose to sides of head. Carefully "color in" these stripes with chocolate sprinkles. Put a Smartie candy on either side of nose for eyes.

10 Using an icing bag fitted with writing tip, pipe melted chocolate to make eyebrows and mouth to complete face.

BIRTHDAY DRUM

Preparation Time
30 minutes
Cooking Time
25 to 30 minutes
Makes
one 8-inch (20 cm)
round cake

Strike up the band with a birthday beat! This fun, drum-shaped cake is really easy to make and ideal for beginners.

Cake:

3/4 cup	granulated sugar	175 mL
1/3 cup	butter or margarine (at room temperature)	75 mL
2	large eggs	2
1 tsp	vanilla extract	5 mL
1-1/2 cups	all-purpose flour	375 mL
2 tsp	baking powder	10 mL
1/4 tsp	salt	1 mL
1/2 cup	milk	125 mL

Buttercream:

3 cups	sifted icing sugar	750 mL
1/2 cup	butter (at room temperature)	125 mL
1/4 cup	milk (approx)	50 mL
	Blue food coloring	
	Red food coloring	

Glacé Icing:

1-1/2 cups	sifted icing sugar (approx)	375 mL
4 tsp	hot water (approx)	20 mL
1/4 tsp	vanilla extract	1 mL

Decoration:

	Jelly licorice allsorts (covered with little beads)	
2	lollipops	2

1 Preheat oven to 350°F (180°C). Have ready a nonstick or lightly greased 8-inch (20 cm) round cake pan.

2 *Cake:* In a medium bowl, beat together sugar and butter until pale yellow and fluffy. Add eggs, one at a time, beating well after each addition. Stir in vanilla extract.

3 In a separate medium bowl, sift together flour, baking powder and salt. With a metal spoon, carefully fold one-third of the flour mixture, followed by one-third of the milk, into creamed mixture. Repeat until all flour mixture and milk are used and a smooth batter is formed.

4 Spoon batter into cake pan, smoothing surface. Bake for 25 to 30 minutes or until cake shrinks away from sides of pan, top springs back when gently pressed, and skewer inserted in center comes out clean. Let cool in pan for 5 minutes, then turn out and let cool completely on a wire rack.

5 *Buttercream:* In a large bowl, beat together icing sugar, butter and enough milk to give a spreading consistency. Transfer 1/2 cup (125 mL) of the Buttercream to a separate bowl. Beat in enough blue food coloring to tint bright blue and set aside. Beat enough red food coloring into remaining larger quantity of Buttercream to tint bright red and set aside.

6 *Glacé Icing:* In a medium bowl, beat together icing sugar, water and vanilla extract until smooth and thick enough to coat back of a spoon, adding more sugar or water, if necessary. Set aside.

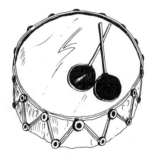

7 *Decoration:* Cut cake in half horizontally and spread base with some of the red Buttercream. Replace top and spread Glacé Icing evenly over top of cake. Spread sides of cake with remaining red Buttercream.

8 Using an icing bag fitted with a small star tip, pipe blue Buttercream in a zigzag pattern from top to bottom on sides of cake. Pipe more blue Buttercream around top edge of cake. Stick a licorice allsort on each point of zigzag. Arrange lollipops on top of cake to resemble drumsticks.

QUICK TIP

If you run out of icing sugar in the middle of decorating a cake, a good substitute can be made by processing some granulated sugar in a coffee grinder or food processor fitted with a metal blade. As a rough guide, 3 cups (750 mL) granulated sugar makes 4 to 4-1/2 cups (1 to 1.125 L) icing sugar.

TREASURE CHEST CAKE

Preparation Time
30 minutes
Cooking Time
50 to 55 minutes
Makes
*one 8-1/2- × 4-1/2-inch
(6 cup/1.5 L) cake*

Give your child a pirate party with this easy "treasure"-filled cake as the centerpiece. Ask the guests to come dressed as pirates, and organize a treasure hunt around the house or backyard.

Cake:

3/4 cup	granulated sugar	175 mL
1 cup	butter or margarine (at room temperature)	250 mL
3	large eggs	3
1 tsp	vanilla extract	5 mL
2 cups	all-purpose flour	500 mL
1 tsp	baking powder	5 mL

Chocolate Buttercream:

2 oz	semi-sweet chocolate (see Quick Tip, p. 141)	60 g
2 cups	icing sugar, sifted	500 mL
1/4 cup	butter (at room temperature)	50 mL
2	egg yolks	2
3 tbsp	milk (approx)	45 mL

Glacé Icing:

1 cup	sifted icing sugar (approx)	250 mL
1 tbsp	hot water (approx)	15 mL
1/4 tsp	vanilla extract	1 mL

Decoration:

	Assorted candies (such as foil-covered chocolate coins, licorice allsorts, Smarties	

1 Preheat oven to 350°F (180°C). Have ready a nonstick or lightly greased 8-1/2-inch × 4-1/2-inch (6 cup/1.5 L) loaf pan.

2 *Cake:* In a medium bowl, beat together sugar and butter until pale yellow and fluffy. Add eggs, one at a time, beating well after each addition. Stir in vanilla extract.

3 In a separate medium bowl, sift together flour and baking powder. With a metal spoon, gradually fold flour mixture into butter mixture until ingredients are well combined.

4 Spoon cake batter into loaf pan and smooth surface. Bake for 30 to 35 minutes until cake shrinks away from sides of pan, top springs back when gently pressed, and skewer inserted in center comes out clean. Let cool in pan for 5 minutes, then turn out and let cool completely on a wire rack.

5 *Chocolate Buttercream:* In a small bowl over a saucepan of gently simmering water or in top of double boiler, melt chocolate, stirring occasionally until smooth. Remove from heat and set aside to cool.

6 In a large bowl, beat together icing sugar, butter, egg yolks and cooled chocolate until smooth. Beat in enough milk to give a spreading consistency and set aside.

7 *Glacé icing:* In a medium bowl, beat together icing sugar, water and vanilla extract until smooth and thick enough to coat back of a spoon, adding more sugar or water, if necessary. Set aside.

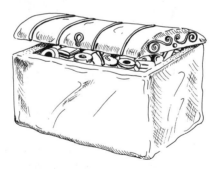

8 *Decoration:* Cut a slice from top of cake to form lid of treasure chest. With a teaspoon, hollow out base slightly by removing a little of the cake. Spread Chocolate Buttercream evenly over sides of base, and top and sides of lid.

9 Using an icing bag fitted with a writing tip, pipe Glacé Icing to make hinges and a keyhole on lid of chest. Pile assorted candies in hollow of base of chest and top with lid at an angle.

FROGGY POND

Preparation Time
35 minutes
Cooking Time
20 to 30 minutes
Makes
*10 to 12 choux
pastry frogs*

These jolly cream-filled frogs sitting on a bright green "pond" are as popular with adults as with children—or maybe I just know really childish adults!

Pond:

1	pkg (6 oz/170 g) lime-flavored jelly powder	1

Pastry:

	Choux Pastry dough (see Strawberry Puff, p. 86)

Filling:

2 cups	whipping cream	500 mL

Glacé Icing:

2 cups	sifted icing sugar (approx)	500 mL
2 tbsp	hot water (approx)	25 mL
1/2 tsp	vanilla extract	2 mL
	Green food coloring	

Decoration:

20 to 24	Smarties candies	20 to 24
1 cup	marzipan	250 mL
	Green food coloring	
	Miniature ornamental flowers	

1 *Pond:* Prepare jelly powder as directed on package. Pour into a very large shallow serving dish or serving tray. Chill until set.

2 Preheat oven to 400°F (200°C). Have ready two nonstick or lightly greased cookie sheets.

3 *Pastry:* Drop 10 to 12 tablespoonfuls of choux pastry, about 2 inches (5 cm) apart, onto cookie sheets. Bake for 20 to 30 minutes or until well risen and golden brown. Make a small horizontal slit near top of each choux puff to allow steam to escape. Let cool completely on a wire rack.

4 *Filling:* In a medium bowl, whip cream until it stands in soft peaks. Set aside.

5 *Glacé Icing:* In a medium bowl, beat together icing sugar, water and vanilla extract until smooth and thick enough to coat back of spoon, adding more sugar or water, if necessary. Beat in enough food coloring to tint icing bright green. Set aside.

6 *Decoration:* Enlarge slits in choux puffs slightly. Using small spoon or piping bag, carefully spoon some of the whipped cream filling into each puff. Using icing bag fitted with a writing tip, pipe Glacé Icing to make a mouth on each puff. Dab a little icing onto two Smarties candies and stick to each puff for eyes.

7 In a medium bowl, knead marzipan with enough food coloring to tint it pale green. Divide marzipan into 20 to 24 even-sized pieces. Shape each piece into a froglike flipper. Arrange marzipan flippers in pairs on Pond and place a choux puff on each pair, using a little icing to hold it in place. Decorate around edge of pond with miniature flowers.

TEDDY BEAR CAKE

Preparation Time
30 minutes
Cooking Time
25 to 30 minutes
Makes
one Teddy Bear Cake

When we were kids, it was a tradition in our family for my mother to make this Teddy Bear Cake for each birthday that came along. Even as the number of candles on the bear's tummy increased with each year, the novelty of this lovely cake never wore off.

Cake:

1-1/2 cups	granulated sugar	375 mL
2/3 cup	butter or margarine (at room temperature)	150 mL
4	large eggs	4
3 cups	all-purpose flour	750 mL
4 tsp	baking powder	20 mL
1/2 tsp	salt	2 mL
1 cup	milk	250 mL
2 tbsp	instant coffee granules	25 mL

Mocha Frosting:

6 oz	semi-sweet chocolate (see Quick Tip, p.141)	175 g
3/4 cup	milk (approx)	175 mL
3 tbsp	instant coffee granules	45 mL
4-1/2 cups	sifted icing sugar	1.125 L
1-1/2 cups	butter (at room temperature)	375 mL
1	large egg	1

Decoration:

	Black licorice shoelaces	
3	Smarties candies	3
1	decorative red bow	1

1 Preheat oven to 350°F (180°C). Have ready two nonstick or lightly greased 8-inch (20 cm) round cake pans and one nonstick or lightly greased 8-inch (20 cm) square cake pan.

2 *Cake:* In a medium bowl, beat together sugar and butter until pale yellow and fluffy. Add eggs, one at a time, beating well after each addition.

---

3 In a separate medium bowl, sift together flour, baking powder and salt. In a small bowl, mix together milk and coffee powder. With a metal spoon, carefully fold one-third of the flour mixture, followed by one-third of the milk, into creamed mixture. Repeat until all flour mixture and milk are used and a smooth batter is formed.

---

4 Divide cake batter between cake pans, making sure cake batter is approximately same depth in each pan and smoothing surfaces. Bake for 25 to 30 minutes or until cakes shrink away from sides of pans, tops spring back when gently pressed, and skewer inserted in centers comes out clean. Let cool in pans for 5 minutes, then turn out and let cool completely on wire racks.

---

5 *Mocha Frosting:* In a small bowl over a saucepan of gently simmering water or in top of double boiler, melt chocolate with milk and coffee powder, stirring occasionally until smooth. Remove from heat and set aside to cool.

---

6 In a large bowl, beat together icing sugar, butter, egg and cooled chocolate mixture until smooth, adding a little more milk, if necessary, to give a spreading consistency. Set aside.

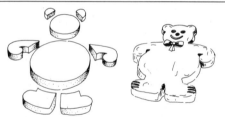

7 *Decoration:* Use one of the round cakes for Teddy Bear's body. Trim other round cake to make a smaller circle for the head and place above body. Cut ear shapes from cake trimmings (see diagram). Cut all pieces of Teddy in half horizontally and spread bases with some of the frosting. Replace tops. Stick body, head and ears together with a little of the Mocha Frosting. Cut two arms and two legs from square cake (see diagram) and stick in place with frosting. Spread top and sides of entire Teddy Bear Cake with remaining frosting.

---

8 Use licorice shoelaces to make Teddy's mouth and claws. Put Smarties candies in place for nose and eyes. Finish with a red bow under Teddy's chin.

QUICK TIP

You can substitute semi-sweet chocolate chips for squares of semi-sweet chocolate in a recipe. One cup (250 mL) chocolate chips weighs about 6 ounces (180 g).

FORT KNOX CAKE

Preparation Time
30 minutes
Cooking Time
55 to 60 minutes
Makes
*one 9- × 5-1/2-inch
(23 × 14 cm) cake*

This large cake is suitable for a big party and it's also one of the simplest to make. If you can't find little flags to decorate the turrets, make your own from scraps of colored paper and wooden toothpicks or Popsicle sticks.

Cake:

2-1/4 cups	granulated sugar	550 mL
1 cup	butter or margarine (at room temperature)	250 mL
6	large eggs	6
4 cups	all-purpose flour	1 L
1/2 cup	unsweetened cocoa powder	125 mL
6 tsp	baking powder	30 mL
1 tsp	salt	5 mL
1-1/2 cups	milk	375 mL

Coffee Buttercream:

7-1/2 cups	sifted icing sugar	1.875 L
1-1/4 cups	butter (at room temperature)	300 mL
8 tbsp	strong black coffee	120 mL
	Water (optional)	

Decoration:

30	chocolate mint sticks (approx)	30
	Miniature ornamental flags	
	Ornamental toy soldiers or cowboys	

1 Preheat oven to 350°F (180°C). Have ready a nonstick or lightly greased and floured 13- × 9- × 2-inch (32 × 23 × 5 cm) baking pan.

2 *Cake:* In a large bowl, beat together sugar and butter until pale yellow and fluffy. Add eggs, one at a time, beating well after each addition.

3 In a separate large bowl, sift together flour, cocoa powder, baking powder and salt. With a metal spoon, carefully fold one-third of the flour mixture, followed by one-third of the milk, into creamed mixture. Repeat until all flour mixture and milk are used and a smooth batter is formed.

4 Spoon cake batter into cake pan and smooth surface. Bake for 55 to 60 minutes, covering cake with foil after 30 minutes, or until cake shrinks from sides of pan, top springs back when gently pressed, and skewer inserted in center comes out clean. Let cool in pan for 5 minutes, then turn out and let cool completely on a wire rack.

5 *Coffee Buttercream:* In a large bowl, beat together icing sugar, butter and coffee until smooth and creamy. Beat in a little water, if necessary, to give a spreading consistency.

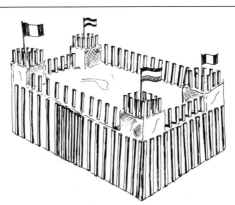

6 *Decoration:* Trim top of cake to level surface, then cut a 2-inch (5 cm) wide slice from one short end of cake. Cut slice into four equal pieces, each about 2 inches (5 cm) square and set aside. Cut remaining cake in half to give two 9- × 5-inch (23 × 12.5 cm) rectangles. Cut each rectangle in half horizontally and sandwich the four layers together with some of the Coffee Buttercream, inverting top layer to give a flat surface. Spread Coffee Buttercream evenly over top and sides of cake.

7 Spread top and sides of the reserved 2-inch (5 cm) squares with Coffee Buttercream and place one square on top of each corner of cake for turrets. Using a toothpick, mark vertical lines on each side of cake to resemble logs.

8 Cut 24 chocolate mint sticks into thirds and stand in frosting evenly around top edge of fort, including turrets. Arrange remaining 6 mint sticks close together on one wall of fort to make a door. Decorate top of fort with flags and toy soldiers or cowboys.

CIRCUS CLOWN CAKES

Preparation Time
30 minutes
Cooking Time
15 to 20 minutes
Makes
6 clown cakes

Instead of baking one large birthday cake, make individual clown cakes for each child. I've suggested one way of decorating the faces, but you could let your imagination run riot and do each one differently.

Cake:

3/4 cup	granulated sugar	175 mL
1/3 cup	butter or margarine (at room temperature)	75 mL
2	large eggs	2
1 tsp	vanilla extract	5 mL
1-1/2 cups	all-purpose flour	375 mL
2 tsp	baking powder	10 mL
1/4 tsp	salt	1 mL
1/2 cup	milk	125 mL

Buttercream:

3 cups	sifted icing sugar	750 mL
1/2 cup	butter (at room temperature)	125 mL
3 tbsp	milk (approx)	45 mL
	Red food coloring	

Filling:

1/4 cup	strawberry jam	50 mL

Decoration:

	Black and red licorice shoelaces	
6	small red candies	6
1 cup	shredded coconut	250 mL
	Yellow food coloring	
6	sugared ice cream cones	6

1 Preheat oven to 350°F (180°C). Have ready a nonstick or lightly greased 12-cup muffin pan.

2 *Cake:* In a medium bowl, beat together sugar and butter until pale yellow and fluffy. Add eggs, one at a time, beating well after each addition. Stir in vanilla extract.

3 In a separate medium bowl, sift together flour, baking powder and salt. With a metal spoon, carefully fold one-third of the flour mixture, followed by one-third of the milk, into creamed mixture. Repeat until all flour mixture and milk are used and a smooth batter is formed.

4 Fill muffin cups two-thirds with batter. Bake for 15 to 20 minutes or until golden brown and risen, and skewer inserted in centers comes out clean. Let cool in muffin pans for 5 minutes, then carefully turn out and let cool on a wire rack.

5 *Buttercream:* In a large bowl, beat together icing sugar, butter and enough milk to give a spreading consistency. Beat in enough food coloring to tint Buttercream pale pink. Set aside.

6 *Filling:* Trim top of each cake to level surface, if necessary. Spread tops of 12 of the cakes with jam and invert remaining cakes on top.

7 *Decoration:* Spread top and sides of cakes evenly with Buttercream. Arrange short lengths of black licorice in cross shapes for clown eyes. Make mouths with red licorice and use red candies for noses.

8 In a small bowl, toss together coconut and food coloring until coconut is tinted pale yellow. Carefully press coconut into Buttercream to make a fringe of hair around sides of heads. Top each cake with an ice cream cone at a jaunty angle for hat.

QUICK TIP

For fast and easy cleanup when making cupcakes or muffins, bake them in paper baking cups standing in an ungreased muffin pan.

PUFFING BILLY

Preparation Time
40 minutes
Cooking Time
20 to 25 minutes
Makes
one 7-inch (18 cm)
long roll

Girls and boys alike will love this cute little train engine. If time is short, buy a jelly roll to decorate instead of baking your own.

Jelly Roll:

3/4 cup	all-purpose flour	175 mL
1 tsp	baking powder	5 mL
1/4 tsp	salt	1 mL
3	large eggs	3
2/3 cup	granulated sugar	150 mL
3 tbsp	warm water	45 mL
	Icing sugar	

Filling:

2/3 cup	strawberry jam	150 mL

Buttercream:

3 cups	sifted icing sugar	750 mL
1/2 cup	butter (at room temperature)	125 mL
3 tbsp	milk (approx)	45 mL
	Green food coloring	

Decoration:

4	Oreo cookies	4
30	Smarties candies (approx)	30
14	coconut licorice allsorts (with licorice in the center)	14
8	Lifesaver candies	8

1 Preheat oven to 375°F (190°C). Line base and sides of a 13- × 9- × 1/2-inch (32 × 23 × 1 cm) jelly roll pan with waxed paper.

2 *Jelly Roll:* Prepare cake batter following method for Spicy Apple Roll (p. 91), omitting cinnamon. Bake and cool as directed.

3 *Filling:* When jelly roll is cold, carefully unroll it and spread with jam. Re-roll cake without tea towel and set aside.

4 *Buttercream:* In a medium bowl, beat together icing sugar, butter and enough milk to give a spreading consistency. Transfer about 1/4 cup (50 mL) of the Buttercream to a separate bowl. Beat enough food coloring into remaining Buttercream to tint it bright green.

5 *Decoration:* Cut a 2-inch (5 cm) wide slice from one end of jelly roll. Cut a semi-circle from slice (see diagram) so slice will stand vertically on top of jelly roll. Using a little Buttercream, stick slice on top of jelly roll at one end to represent cab of engine. Spread front end of engine with white Buttercream. Cover rest of cake evenly with green Buttercream.

6 Stick two Oreo cookies on each side towards rear of engine for wheels. Decorate top of cab with Smarties candies.

7 Using a little leftover Buttercream, stick 8 coconut licorice allsorts together in two columns of 4, and stick on top of engine for funnels. Stick 3 licorice allsorts on each side of base of engine for small wheels. Decorate each side of engine with 4 Lifesaver candies.

RECIPE INDEX

SUBJECT INDEX

Coffee crunch cake, 62
Cookie cutters, 12
Cookies:
    almond orange icebox, 41
    basic icebox, 40
    brandy snaps, 121
    cherry fingers, 32
    chocolate mint pinwheel icebox, 42
    chocolate stuff, 37
    crisp, 80
    fruit 'n' spice icebox, 41
    ginger nuts, 33
    icebox, 40
    lemon and cardamom filigree, 38
    one pot tutti fruttis, 64
    orange and walnut macaroons, 39
    peanut bars, 36
    pud, Gooey, 29
    rock cakes, 35
    with blue cheese, Sour cream, 104
Cream, 14
Creamy strawberry tartlets, 98
Crunchy zucchini loaf, 47
Cumin, 14
Cupboard storage:
    dry goods, 21
    miscellaneous, 21

Danish apple cake, 126
Date and ginger loaf, 52
Definitive chocolate chunk cookie,
    The, 34

Eggs, 14
Emergency supplies:
    cupboard, 29
    gooey cookie pud, 29
    refrigerator, 29
    trifle, 29
Extracts, 15

Feta cheese, 15
Feta cheese pie, 123
First Aid:
    cakes, 26
    cookies, 25
    fruit bread and cakes, 28
    jelly roll, 26
    meringues, 27
    pastry, 28
    quick breads and muffins, 27
    tea biscuits, 27
Flour:
    all-purpose, 15
    semolina, 15
    whole wheat, 15
Fluffy seafood quiches, 103
Food coloring, 15

Fort Knox cake, 142
Freezing foods:
    how to thaw, 23
    quick-freezing, 22
    storage time, 23
Froggy pond, 138
Fruit:
    dried, 46
    loaf, Rich, 48
Fruit 'n' nut bars, 61
Fruit 'n' spice icebox cookies, 41

Garam masala, 15
Ginger nuts, 33
Glazed orange cake, 128
Glazed walnut apricot cake, 94
Glossary of cooking terms, 18
Good-for-you bars, 77
Gooey chewy bars, 63
Gooey chocolate cherry cake, 96
Gooey cookie pud, 29

Ham and mustard tea biscuits, 56
Ham and watercress strudel, 111
Herbs, 15

Icebox cookies:
    almond orange, 41
    basic, 40
    chocolate mint pinwheel, 42
    fruit 'n' spice, 41
Italian pizza tea bread, 49

Janhagel, 127
Jelly roll, 26

Lemon and blueberry crunch, 56
Lemon and cardamom filigree cookies,
    38
Lemon and cherry tea biscuits, 55

Malted slab cake, 81
Margarine, 15
Measurement:
    brown sugar, 17
    dry ingredients, 17
    fats, 17
    fats for melting, 17
    liquids, 17
    syrup and honey, 17
Meringues, 27
Milk, 15
Muffins, 73
Mushroom toasts, 113

No bake fruity bars, 65
Nutmeg, 15
Nuts, 16

One pot tutti fruttis, 64

If you enjoyed Baker's Secret, why not give a copy to a friend or treat yourself to another one of our bestselling cookbooks, Light & Easy Choices by Kay Spicer. Available at most bookstores or order directly from Grosvenor House Press. A convenient order form is supplied below:

☐ Yes. I would like to order:

_____ Baker's Secret
       (copies)

_____ Light & Easy Choices
       (copies)

Enclosed is $ _____ ($12.95 each, plus $1.50 per book shipping and handling.)

Make cheque or money order payable to:

Grosvenor House Press Inc.
111 Queen Street East, Suite 375
Toronto, Ontario M5C 1S2

☐ Visa   ☐ MasterCard

Account Number _____
Name _____
Address _____
_____
_____ Postal Code _____
Telephone Number _____
Expiry Date _____
Signature _____

If you enjoyed Baker's Secret, why not give a copy to a friend or treat yourself to another one of our bestselling cookbooks, Light & Easy Choices by Kay Spicer. Available at most bookstores or order directly from Grosvenor House Press. A convenient order form is supplied below:

☐ Yes. I would like to order:

_____ Baker's Secret
(copies)

_____ Light & Easy Choices
(copies)

Enclosed is $ _____ ($12.95 each, plus $1.50 per book shipping and handling.)

Make cheque or money order payable to:

Grosvenor House Press Inc.
111 Queen Street East, Suite 375
Toronto, Ontario M5C 1S2

☐ Visa   ☐ MasterCard

Account Number _____

Name _____

Address _____

_____ Postal Code _____

Telephone Number _____

Expiry Date _____

Signature _____

If you enjoyed Baker's Secret, why not give a copy to a friend or treat yourself to another one of our bestselling cookbooks, Light & Easy Choices by Kay Spicer. Available at most bookstores or order directly from Grosvenor House Press. A convenient order form is supplied below:

☐ Yes. I would like to order:

_____ Baker's Secret
    (copies)

_____ Light & Easy Choices
    (copies)

Enclosed is $ _____ ($12.95 each, plus $1.50 per book shipping and handling.)

Make cheque or money order payable to:

Grosvenor House Press Inc.
111 Queen Street East, Suite 375
Toronto, Ontario M5C 1S2

☐ Visa   ☐ MasterCard

Account Number _____
Name _____
Address _____
_____
_____ Postal Code _____
Telephone Number _____
Expiry Date _____
Signature _____